NATIONAL TRUST

Book of Biscuits

NATIONAL TRUST
Book of Biscuits

Linda Collister

National Trust

Published by National Trust Books

An imprint of HarperCollins Publishers, 1 London Bridge Street, London SE1 9GF www.harpercollins.co.uk

HarperCollins Publishers, Macken House, 39/40 Mayor Street Upper, Dublin 1, D01 C9W8, Ireland

First published 2026

© National Trust Books 2026

Text © Linda Collister

Illustrations © Louise Morgan

The quotation on page 8 is from *Notes From A Small Island* by Bill Bryson published by Doubleday. Copyright © Bill Bryson, 2015. Reprinted by permission of The Random House Group Limited.

ISBN 978-0-00-877236-9

10 9 8 7 6 5 4 3 2 1

All rights reserved. No part of this publication may be reproduced, stored in a retrieval system, or transmitted, in any form or by any means, electronic, mechanical, photocopying, recording or otherwise without the prior permission in writing of the publisher and copyright owners.

Without limiting the exclusive rights of any author, contributor or the publisher of this publication, any unauthorised use of this publication to train generative artificial intelligence (AI) technologies is expressly prohibited. HarperCollins also exercise their rights under Article 4(3) of the Digital Single Market Directive 2019/790 and expressly reserve this publication from the text and data mining exception.

The contents of this publication are believed correct at the time of printing. Nevertheless, the publisher can accept no responsibility for errors or omissions, changes in the detail given or for any expense or loss thereby caused.

A catalogue record for this book is available from the British Library.

Printed in India by Multivista Global Pvt. Ltd

If you would like to comment on any aspect of this book, please contact us at the above address or national.trust@harpercollins.co.uk

National Trust publications are available at National Trust shops or online at nationaltrustbooks.co.uk

This book contains FSC™ certified paper and other controlled sources to ensure responsible forest management.

For more information visit: www.harpercollins.co.uk/green

Contents

Introduction	6
Good Things to Know	9
1: Nice and Easy	13
2: All About Chocolate	45
3: Something Fancy	69
4: Squares and Bars	101
5: Biscotti	121
6: Savoury	135
Index	154
Acknowledgements	160

Introduction

The British are indisputably a nation of biscuit lovers, leading the world in biscuit consumption. But what is it that makes that combination of crisp and sweet so irresistible – especially when paired with a cup of tea? The 1970s advertising slogan, 'a drink's too wet without one', is a sentiment that many of us can relate to.

During the Second World War, with the rationing of most foodstuffs, including sugar, flour, eggs and butter, home baking was restricted. Heavily sweetened tea was also out. The government quickly realised that allowing manufacturers enough sugar to make sweet biscuits could supply a much-needed boost to morale and energy. Soon canteens and mobile kitchens, run by the Women's Voluntary Service, were distributing that vital pick-me-up – tea and biscuits.

The amazing variety of biscuits we enjoy today would have been unimaginable to Britain's early biscuit lovers. The English word 'biscuit' first appeared in the fourteenth century: derived from the Latin *panis biscotus* – literally 'bread twice cooked' – these biscuits were slightly stale rich white bread or rolls cut into thick slices, sprinkled with sugar and spices, then baked a second time at the end of the day in the cooling ovens. They must have been dry and crisp and rusk-like, in fact, rather like modern-day *biscotti*, eaten dipped into wine or hot drinks.

Not all early biscuits were sweet. Ship's biscuit, or hard tack, thick slabs of plain, paste-like dough, was baked up to four times until hard and dry enough to discourage weevils. On long sea voyages the biscuit was soaked and used as the base of stews and soups. Finer crackers, such as Bath Olivers and Jacob's Cream Crackers (see a homemade variation on page 152), were created in the eighteenth and nineteenth centuries; these were eaten with cheeses or with wine.

By the seventeenth century, rich shortbread-like doughs were flavoured with caraway seeds and formed into intricate pretzel-like knots or plaits, sometimes called jumballs or gumballs, and regarded as breath fresheners or aids to digestion as much as sweet treats. One extravagant recipe in *Arcana Fairfaxiana* (a manuscript volume of medical recipes and household advice) calls for rosewater, mace, beaten eggs, sugar and flour.

In 1800, a relatively cheap type of sugar – extracted from beets – was developed in a refinery in Silesia, central Europe; the emperor Napoleon was responsible for introducing its mass production in Europe. Around the same time, technological advances made it easier to produce large quantities of white flour. These developments coincided with the Industrial Revolution and lucrative, factory-like bakeries. Crawford's (in Leith), Huntley and Palmers (in Reading) and Carr's (in Carlisle) were household names by the 1850s.

For workers on long shifts, manufactured biscuits, along with sweet tea, were a readily available and inexpensive source of energy – while first-class train travellers could relax with tea and Huntley and Palmers biscuits in special 'railway' packs. However, afternoon tea with homemade cakes and biscuits was still a ritual for better-off Victorians who possessed their own ovens (and their own cooks).

There's a biscuit for every occasion and recipes from around the world. In this book you can explore the many ways spices are used in biscuits, from ginger snaps and gingerbreads to German lebkuchen. There are also white chocolate, pine nut and chilli cookies and wheaten biscuits with garam masala. Nuts are another popular ingredient. Pistachios, walnuts and hazelnuts are used in several recipes, while ground almonds feature in the many variations of macaroons – from Italian ricciarelli to French sandwiched style. If you like a filling, oaty snack, you'll find recipes for oat and raisin cookies, flapjacks and granola bars. And if you can never resist a chocolate biscuit, turn to pages 46–67 for a chapter that's all about chocolate. American-style cookies, quite sweet and chewy (perfect for ice-cream sandwiches), are just as much at home in this book as our traditional and much-loved buttery Scottish shortbread.

The American author Bill Bryson paid homage to our culinary heritage in *Notes from a Small Island* when he asked: 'What other nation in the world could possibly have given us William Shakespeare, pork pies, Christopher Wren, Windsor Great Park, the Open University, Gardeners' Question Time and the chocolate digestive biscuit?' (See page 20 for a delicious take on this popular classic.) Biscuits are not only the nation's favourite teatime treat, they are a British cultural icon.

Most biscuits are simple, yet simply delicious. They really are perfect for when you need a tea-break treat to share with work colleagues, friends and family – and nothing beats homemade.

Good Things to Know

Homemade biscuits are a simple pleasure needing just a few basic ingredients, very little effort and some inexpensive equipment. The keys to success are to read the recipe through before starting and to use good-quality materials and bakeware. Here are some pointers to successful baking.

• All spoon measurements are level, unless specified otherwise. 1 teaspoon = 5ml; 1 tablespoon = 15ml.

• Eggs are always medium, free range and normally used at room temperature.

• Butter is unsalted. Plant butter should be a block, not spread.

• Milk is semi-skimmed or whole (full fat).

• Citrus zest is always from unwaxed fruit, organic if possible.

• Porridge oats should be the traditional variety, not instant or jumbo oats.

• (GF) denotes a gluten-free recipe. Check ingredient packaging carefully on grain products such as oats and oatmeal to ensure they are gluten free, as some products may be contaminated with other grains.

• Gluten-free flour blends are readily available – the best ones are labelled 'all-purpose' or 'for biscuits and shortcrust pastry making'; they are usually a mix of brown and white rice flours, maize starch and flour, tapioca starch and buckwheat flour. Some blends include binders – such as guar gum or xanthan gum – and work better for sponges and bread doughs; some blends also have stronger, less neutral flavours than others and can vary in their absorption of moisture. It is not always possible to substitute like with like and so some experimentation may be needed.

• Look for dark chocolate with around 70 per cent cocoa solids, or as specified in the recipe. Avoid 'chocolate flavour cake covering' as it doesn't taste or work as well as chocolate itself.

• To melt chocolate, break or chop it into even-sized pieces and put into a heatproof bowl. Set over a pan of steaming hot but not boiling water; don't let the base of the bowl touch the water. Leave to melt gently, stirring from time to time. Remove the bowl from the heat and stir gently until smooth. Alternatively, melt in the microwave on medium power in 20- to 30-second bursts, stirring occasionally, until smooth.

• Nuts are a key ingredient for many recipes; their flavour will determine the final result. Make sure they are as fresh as possible; the oils in them will turn rancid in only a few weeks once the pack is opened. It is best to store opened packs in the freezer.

• Spices lose their flavour and aroma and become stale, so check the use-by dates.

• The most basic kitchen equipment needed, along with kitchen scales, is a mixing bowl, wooden spoon, at least one good heavy-duty baking sheet and a wire cooling rack. For some recipes an electric mixer or whisk and a food processor will speed up the beating or chopping. Some recipes need a rolling pin. An airtight container for storing baked biscuits is essential. Round or fluted biscuit cutters may be required for some recipes, though the rim of a glass can be used instead.

• It is a good idea to line your baking sheet with non-stick baking paper to avoid your biscuits sticking or burning. Lightly grease the baking sheet first with a small amount of butter or oil.

- Make sure you space out the biscuits on the baking sheets to allow room for spreading during baking. If baking in batches, allow the sheets to cool down before adding a second batch.

- Oven temperatures and times are for conventional ovens; check your oven handbook for details on baking with a fan oven as the temperatures and/or timings may differ. If in doubt, bake a couple of biscuits first before putting the entire batch in the oven.

- Always preheat the oven so that it is the correct temperature when you are ready to bake.

- To keep a cylinder or log of dough in good shape in the fridge or freezer, wrap it tightly in baking paper, then place it in the cardboard inner tube from a roll of kitchen paper, cut open along its length.

- It is worth getting an oven thermometer to check how your oven is behaving – each oven is different, and thermostats can be unreliable. Some shelf positions may work better than others, and you will need to know how to avoid any hot spots, and when to rotate the baking sheets to ensure even baking. Biscuits cook in a matter of minutes and the cooking times given in this book are guidelines: you will need to trust your knowledge and senses.

Chapter 1
Nice and Easy

Anzac Biscuits

These delicious biscuits, with crisp edges and chewy centres, are made by the simple 'melt and mix' method. They are often made for Anzac Day on 25 April, the anniversary of the arrival of the ANZACs (Australian and New Zealand Army Corps) at Gallipoli in 1915. The biscuits, made without eggs so that they kept for longer, were reportedly first baked by wives, mothers and sisters of ANZAC soldiers and sent to the troops by sea in special metal tins.

Makes about 26

40g golden syrup
125g unsalted butter or plant butter
1 tsp bicarbonate of soda
2 tbsp boiling water

100g porridge oats
100g plain flour
A large pinch of salt
100g caster sugar
85g desiccated coconut

Line two or three baking sheets with baking paper. Preheat the oven to 180°C.

Weigh the golden syrup and butter into a small saucepan and melt gently over a low heat, stirring with a wooden spoon. Remove from the heat.

Dissolve the bicarbonate of soda in the boiling water in a small cup, then stir it into the melted mixture.

Put the oats, flour, salt, sugar and coconut into a large mixing bowl and mix well with a wooden spoon, then add the melted mixture and stir until thoroughly combined.

Using a tablespoon measure, scoop out a level tablespoon of the mixture, roll it between your hands to make a neat ball, then place on a lined baking sheet. Repeat with the remaining mixture, spacing the balls well apart to allow for spreading.

Bake for 12–14 minutes until a deep golden colour – check after 10 minutes and rotate the sheets so the biscuits colour evenly. Leave to firm up for a couple of minutes, then transfer to a wire rack to cool.

When completely cold, store in an airtight container and eat within a week.

Cinnamon Sandies

Toasted almonds transform a simple combination of flour, butter, sugar and cinnamon into a rich and rather sophisticated sandy-textured biscuit. The dough is formed into a log, chilled and cut into slices before baking.

Makes 12

65g blanched almonds
150g plain flour
A large pinch of salt
¼ tsp baking powder
1 tsp ground cinnamon

100g unsalted butter or plant butter, softened
60g caster sugar
Icing sugar for dusting

Line two baking sheets with baking paper. Preheat the oven to 180°C.

Put all but 12 of the almonds into an ovenproof dish – reserve the remaining almonds to decorate the biscuits – and toast in the oven for about 10–14 minutes until lightly browned. Leave to cool; you can turn off the oven for now.

Tip the cooled almonds into a food processor. Add the flour, salt, baking powder and cinnamon and process to a fairly fine, sandy powder.

Put the butter and sugar into a mixing bowl and beat well until creamy. Add the flour mixture and mix to combine, then use your hands to bring the mixture together.

Turn out the dough onto a large sheet of baking paper and shape into a neat log about 5cm across and 12cm long. Wrap tightly and chill for about 15 minutes until firm but not rock-hard. At this point the log, very well wrapped (see page 11), can be kept in the fridge for up to 5 days or frozen for up to a month. Bring back to a firm texture before continuing.

Reheat the oven to 180°C. Cut the log into 12 slices, 1cm thick. Arrange well apart on the lined baking sheets. Press a whole almond into the centre of each slice, then bake for about 20 minutes until a light golden colour, with slightly darker edges. Leave to firm up for 5 minutes, then transfer to a wire rack to cool.

When completely cold, dust with icing sugar. Store in an airtight container and eat within a week.

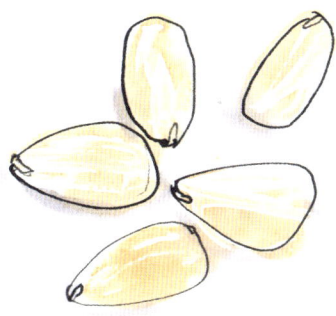

Cornish Fairings

Seasonal country fairs, where workers were hired, livestock bought and sold, and market goods traded, have been operating since the twelfth century. Honey and spice cakes were sold as edible souvenirs and by the mid-nineteenth century these had evolved in the West Country to spicy biscuits, which were simpler to produce by the dozen. This version, with a slightly chewy texture and flavoured with chopped candied lemon and orange peel along with the spices, is a traditional favourite in Cornwall.

Makes 18

100g plain flour
1 tbsp cut mixed peel
A large pinch of salt
1 tsp baking powder
½ tsp bicarbonate of soda
½ tsp ground mixed spice

1 tsp ground ginger
40g caster sugar
50g unsalted butter or plant butter, chilled and diced
50g golden syrup

Line two baking sheets with baking paper. Preheat the oven to 190°C.

Combine a teaspoon of the weighed flour with the mixed peel and chop even finer. Set aside.

Sift the remaining flour, salt, baking powder, bicarbonate of soda, mixed spice, ginger and sugar into a mixing bowl. Stir in the peel and flour mixture, then add the diced butter. Toss until coated, then rub the butter into the flour mixture between the tips of your fingers, or cut in with a metal pastry blender, until the mixture looks like breadcrumbs. Make a well in the centre of the mixture.

Weigh the golden syrup into a small pan and warm gently, just until the syrup is fluid but not hot, then pour into the well. Using a wooden spoon, mix everything together to make a stiff dough.

Pull off small pieces of dough and roll between your hands to make 18 cherry-sized balls. Arrange on the lined baking sheets, spacing them well apart to allow for spreading.

Bake for 7–9 minutes until golden brown – watch them carefully and rotate the sheets halfway through baking so they colour evenly. Leave to firm up for a couple of minutes, then transfer to a wire rack to cool.

When completely cold, store in an airtight container and eat within a week.

Wheaten Biscuits

Digestive biscuits are the best-selling biscuits in the UK and regularly top the lists of the nation's favourite biscuits. They have a long history: the first recipe, developed by two Scottish doctors, included bicarbonate of soda, an antacid, and in 1876 Huntley and Palmers advertised them for sale in chemists as an aid to digestion. The now-popular McVitie's biscuit followed in 1892, and their chocolate-coated version, described by writer Bill Bryson as a masterpiece, was originally produced in 1925.

This recipe makes plain and simple biscuits that are slightly more coarse and less sweet than supermarket varieties but still deliciously crunchy. As a variation, try finishing them with your favourite chocolate, or make a lightly spiced savoury version to eat with cheese, dips or smoked fish.

Wheatgerm and bran mix is available from health food and wholefood shops, and is sometimes found in the cereal or breadmaking sections of supermarkets.

Makes about 16

150g plain wholemeal flour
150g fine oatmeal
10g wheatgerm and bran mix
¼ tsp salt
1 tsp baking powder

75g dark muscovado sugar, sieved
150g unsalted butter or plant butter, chilled and diced
1–2 tbsp milk, oat milk or water

To make in a food processor: put the flour, oatmeal, wheatgerm and bran mix, salt, baking powder and sugar into the processor bowl and pulse until combined. Add the butter and process until the mixture looks like sandy crumbs. With the machine running, add the liquid a tablespoon at a time through the feed tube to bring the mixture together into a ball of firm but not dry dough.

To make in a mixing bowl: combine all the dry ingredients and mix well. Add the butter and toss until coated, then rub in between the tips of your fingers until the mixture looks like sandy crumbs. Using a round-bladed knife, stir in enough liquid to make a firm ball of dough.

Turn out the dough onto a sheet of baking paper and flatten to a thick disc. Cover with a second sheet of baking paper and chill for about 20 minutes until firm.

Meanwhile, preheat the oven to 190°C and line two baking sheets with baking paper.

Roll out the dough between the two sheets of baking paper (this avoids using extra flour, which could make the biscuits dry) to 4mm thick – slightly thicker than a pound coin. Stamp out rounds using a 7cm plain round cutter and arrange slightly apart on the lined baking sheets. Gather up the trimmings, gently knead them together, then roll out again and cut more rounds. Prick each round several times with a fork, then bake for 11–15 minutes until firm and golden with slightly darker edges.

Leave to firm up for 3 minutes, then transfer to a wire rack to cool.

When completely cold, store in an airtight container and eat within a week.

Chocolate Biscuits

Melt 150g of good-quality milk, white or dark chocolate (see page 10), then spread over (or dip) half of each cold biscuit in the melted chocolate and leave to set on baking paper.

Savoury Biscuits

Make up the recipe on the previous page, but reduce the sugar to 50g and add an extra ¼ teaspoon salt, or sea salt flakes, to taste, plus ½ teaspoon garam masala and ⅛–¼ teaspoon Kashmiri or other chilli powder, to taste.

Cragside Crackles

These warmly spiced oaty biscuits come highly recommended by regulars to the tea-room at Cragside, a National Trust property near Rothbury in Northumberland.

The house and estate were home to Margaret and William Armstrong; the house was designed by Norman Shaw and is recognised as a masterpiece of Victorian Tudor Revival architecture. William was a scientist, engineer and inventor, notably in the field of hydraulics – he built Newcastle's Swing Bridge and the mechanism that operates Tower Bridge in London. His house was the first in the world to be lit by hydroelectric power.

These biscuits were created by the chefs in the tea-room at Cragside, who were inspired by Lord Armstrong's photos of electric currents passing through water: the bicarbonate of soda in the mixture helps the dough to split as it bakes for a crackle effect and the simple glaze adds the electrifying sparkle.

Makes 16–18

185g plain flour, plus extra for dusting
¼ tsp salt
½ tsp bicarbonate of soda
1 tsp ground ginger
½ tsp ground mixed spice
¾ tsp ground cinnamon
65g porridge oats
135g unsalted butter, chilled and diced

75g caster sugar
75g light muscovado sugar
1 medium egg, at room temperature, beaten
½ tsp vanilla extract

To glaze

1 egg white
About 20g caster sugar

Line two or three baking sheets with baking paper. Preheat the oven to 180°C.

Sift the flour, salt, bicarbonate of soda, ginger, mixed spice and cinnamon into a large mixing bowl. Stir in the oats, then add the butter and rub in using your fingertips, or cut in with a metal pastry blender, until the mixture looks like breadcrumbs. Stir in both sugars, then make a well in the mixture and pour in the beaten egg and vanilla.

Mix everything together using a round-bladed knife, then use your hands to bring the mixture together to form a soft but not sticky dough.

Turn out onto a lightly floured worktop and roll out to about 4mm thick. Stamp out rounds using a 7cm plain round cutter, then gather up the trimmings, roll out again and cut more rounds. Set the rounds well apart on the lined baking sheets – they will spread at least 2cm.

For the glaze, beat the egg white with a fork until frothy, then brush over the biscuits. Sprinkle with caster sugar as evenly as possible, then bake for about 15–17 minutes until golden and firm. Check after 10 minutes and rotate the baking sheets so the biscuits colour evenly. Leave to firm up for a couple of minutes, then transfer to a wire rack to cool.

When completely cold, store in an airtight container and eat within a week.

French Sablés

The glass counters of the best patisseries and boulangeries in Normandy and Brittany are always topped with prettily wrapped bags of these glossy, vanilla-scented discs, made from the local unsalted butter and enriched with egg yolks: the traditional Norman recipe dates back to the nineteenth century. The biscuits have a crisp, sandy texture and rich, buttery taste, and are easy to make in a food processor.

Makes about 10

200g plain flour, plus extra for dusting
¼ tsp salt
80g icing sugar
135g unsalted butter, chilled and diced

3 egg yolks
½ tsp vanilla extract

To glaze
1 egg, beaten

Line two baking sheets with baking paper.

Put the flour, salt and sugar into the bowl of a food processor and pulse until combined, or sift into a large mixing bowl. Add the butter and process, or rub in using your fingertips, until the mixture looks like fine crumbs.

Add the egg yolks and vanilla to the mixture. In the processor, pulse until the mixture comes together to make a ball of dough. Or, in a mixing bowl, stir in using a round-bladed knife, then use your hands to bring the dough together into a ball.

Turn out onto a sheet of baking paper and gently flatten to a disc about 4cm thick, then wrap and chill for about 15 minutes or until firm but not rock-hard.

Lightly flour a worktop and roll out the dough to about 5mm thick. Stamp out rounds using an 8cm round fluted cutter. Gather up the trimmings and gently knead them together, then roll out again and cut more rounds.

Arrange the rounds slightly apart on the lined baking sheets, then brush very lightly with beaten egg to glaze. Chill for 15 minutes. Meanwhile, preheat the oven to 180°C.

Brush the rounds a second time with the beaten egg. Prick all over with a fork, then drag the back of the fork across the top of the biscuits to make a neat criss-cross pattern.

Bake for 12–15 minutes or until a rich golden colour. Leave to firm up for 2 minutes, then transfer to a wire rack to cool.

When completely cold, store in an airtight container and eat within a week.

Jammy Thumbprints

Rich, crumbly, great fun to make and a joy to eat! The simple rubbed-in dough mixture is shaped into balls and given a thumbprint centre filled with a favourite jam.

Makes 16

225g plain flour
25g porridge oats
¼ tsp salt
100g caster sugar
1½ tsp baking powder

150g unsalted butter, chilled and diced
1 medium egg, plus 1 egg yolk
About 3 tbsp good raspberry or strawberry jam

Line two baking sheets with baking paper. Preheat the oven to 200°C.

Put the flour, oats, salt, sugar and baking powder into a large mixing bowl and mix well.

Add the butter, toss until coated, then rub into the floury mixture between the tips of your fingers, or cut in with a metal pastry blender, until the mixture looks like coarse breadcrumbs.

Beat the whole egg with the yolk, then add to the bowl and stir into the dry ingredients using a wooden spoon until everything starts to come together. Using your hands, gently and briefly knead the mixture to make a fairly firm ball of dough.

Divide the dough into 16 equal pieces, then roll each piece between your hands to make a ball. Set the balls on the lined baking sheets at least 5cm apart to allow for spreading, then press your floured thumb into the middle of each ball to make a good hollow. Spoon about ½ teaspoon of jam into each hollow, then bake for about 15 minutes until golden.

Leave to firm up for about 10 minutes, then carefully transfer to a wire rack to cool – the jam will be very hot.

When completely cold, store in an airtight container and eat within 5 days.

Lemon Poppy Seed Cookies

These cookies use olive oil rather than butter: the warm aromatic flavour marries well with earthy poppy seeds. It's best to use a mild, fruity oil rather than a pungent or peppery one, and to open a fresh pack of poppy seeds: they need to be used fresh as they rapidly stale once exposed to the air; store the rest of the pack tightly wrapped in the freezer.

Makes 16

70g caster sugar
Finely grated zest of 1 unwaxed lemon
125g plain flour, plus extra for dusting
A large pinch of salt
½ tsp baking powder
1 tbsp poppy seeds
1 medium egg
2½ tbsp olive oil
½ tsp lemon juice or limoncello liqueur

Line two baking sheets with baking paper.

Put the sugar into a mixing bowl, add the lemon zest and briefly rub the two together with your fingertips to release the fragrant oils. Sift the flour, salt and baking powder into the bowl, add the poppy seeds and mix thoroughly with a wooden spoon. Make a well in the centre of the mixture.

Crack the egg into a small bowl, add the oil and lemon juice or limoncello and beat with a fork until combined. Pour into the well in the flour mixture and mix everything together with a wooden spoon to make a soft and slightly sticky dough. Cover the bowl and chill for about 30 minutes until the dough is firm enough to hold a shape.

Towards the end of this time, preheat the oven to 180°C.

Divide the dough into 16 equal pieces, then lightly flour your hands and roll each piece between your hands to make cherry-sized balls. Arrange well apart on the lined baking sheets and bake for about 10–13 minutes until pale gold with slightly darker edges.

Leave to firm up for a couple of minutes, then transfer to a wire rack to cool.

When completely cold, store in an airtight container and eat within 5 days.

Maple Pecan Cookies

Rich, crumbly and buttery, these cookies get their pecan-pie flavour (even better the next day) from real maple syrup along with toasted nuts.

The dough needs to be thoroughly chilled before baking: at least 4 hours (or up to 5 days) well wrapped in the fridge, or frozen for a month then thawed overnight in the fridge. This also means you can slice off and bake a few cookies at a time.

Makes 30

175g pecan pieces or halves
100g pure maple syrup
225g unsalted butter or plant butter, softened

50g light muscovado sugar
250g plain flour
¼ tsp salt

Preheat the oven to 170°C.

Tip 100g of the nuts into an ovenproof dish and toast in the oven for 3–4 minutes until slightly darker in colour. Leave to cool; turn off the oven for now.

Meanwhile, measure the maple syrup into a small saucepan, set over a low–medium heat and leave to simmer gently until reduced to half its original volume. Transfer the thickened syrup to a large mixing bowl and leave to cool for a couple of minutes.

Add the butter and sugar to the bowl and beat with a wooden spoon for a few minutes until the mixture is lump-free and very creamy.

Transfer the cooled pecans to a food processor and grind to a coarse sandy texture with a few slightly larger pieces – you don't want a flour-like or oily texture caused by overprocessing. Add to the creamed mixture along with the flour and salt; mix thoroughly to make a slightly soft and sticky dough.

Turn out onto a worktop and shape the mixture to form a log about 5cm across and 30cm long – it doesn't need to be too neat. Avoid using any extra flour as it will make it difficult for the nut coating to adhere.

Chop the remaining 75g nuts by hand or in a food processor until they are like fine gravel, then scatter them over a large sheet of baking paper. Lift the log onto the paper and gently roll it until the sides are completely coated in nuts. Gently shape into a neat cylinder 5cm across and 30cm long, then wrap tightly in the baking paper. Leave to chill until solid – at least 4 hours. If leaving for longer, or freezing, transfer to a reusable freezer bag or storage container.

When ready to bake, reheat the oven to 170°C and line two baking sheets with baking paper. Cut the log into 1cm slices and arrange on the baking sheets, setting the slices slightly apart to allow for spreading.

Bake for about 15–18 minutes until just firm and lightly golden with slightly darker edges. Leave to firm up for 3–4 minutes, then transfer to a wire rack to cool.

When completely cold, store in an airtight container and eat within 5 days.

Oat and Raisin Cookies

An old recipe that's both simple and adaptable: toasting the oats adds a deep flavour; dark muscovado sugar has a richer flavour than the lighter variety; the raisins can be replaced with soft-dried sour cherries or cranberries, or even chocolate chips. The spices can be omitted, or slightly increased; for a chunky texture you can add walnut pieces. Slight underbaking will give chewier cookies, while adding a minute or two will make them crunchier, so bake a couple of cookies first to decide which you prefer.

Makes about 36

270g porridge oats
225g unsalted butter, softened
175g dark or light muscovado sugar
50g caster sugar
2 medium eggs
1 tsp vanilla extract

185g plain flour
¼ tsp salt
1 tsp bicarbonate of soda
½ tsp ground cinnamon
1 tsp ground mixed spice
110g raisins
100g walnut pieces (optional)

Line two or three baking sheets with baking paper. Preheat the oven to 180°C.

Tip the oats into a large ovenproof dish and toast in the oven until very lightly coloured, about 5 minutes. Leave to cool.

Meanwhile, beat the butter with the sugars in a large bowl, using a wooden spoon or electric mixer, until smooth and creamy. Beat the eggs with the vanilla and beat into the mixture in three batches, scraping down the sides of the bowl from time to time.

Sift the flour, salt, bicarbonate of soda and spices into the bowl and mix with a wooden spoon. Add the oats and raisins (and nuts, if using) and mix well – the mixture will be stiff and heavy, but it is important that the ingredients are thoroughly combined: the aim is that each cookie has a raisin in every bite.

Using a tablespoon measure, scoop the mixture onto the lined baking sheets, spacing the cookies well apart to allow for spreading. Slightly flatten each one so they are about 5cm across.

Bake for 12–14 minutes until the centres no longer look damp and the edges are starting to brown. Leave to firm up for a couple of minutes, then transfer to a wire rack to cool.

When completely cold, store in an airtight container and eat within 5 days.

Old-fashioned Double Ginger Snaps

A well-loved family favourite recipe dating back to the 1890s, made with both ground ginger and sticky preserved stem ginger. It is made by the simple 'melt and mix' method: the golden syrup is warmed with the butter, making it easy to combine with the dry ingredients. The distinctive crackle effect is made by the bicarbonate of soda; the snap depends on the baking time.

Makes 24

85g golden syrup
110g unsalted butter, diced
About 45g (2–3 pieces) drained stem ginger, finely chopped, or ready-chopped glacé ginger
340g self-raising flour, plus extra for dusting
¼ tsp salt
1 tbsp ground ginger
1 tsp bicarbonate of soda
200g caster sugar
1 medium egg, beaten

Line two or three baking sheets with baking paper. Preheat the oven to 170°C.

Weigh the golden syrup, butter and stem or glacé ginger into a small saucepan and set over a low heat. Stir with a wooden spoon until the butter has melted; set aside.

Sift the flour, salt, ground ginger and bicarbonate of soda into a large mixing bowl. Stir in the sugar, then add the butter and syrup mixture and the beaten egg; mix everything together with a wooden spoon to make a firm dough.

Lightly flour your hands and roll the dough into 24 walnut-sized balls. Arrange them well apart on the lined baking sheets to allow for spreading, then slightly flatten each ball – this will help them to bake evenly.

Bake for 15–20 minutes until a good golden brown – check halfway through and rotate the baking sheets so the biscuits colour evenly. The shorter baking time will result in a chewy biscuit; for a crisper one bake a bit longer (it is worth baking a couple first as a test). Leave to firm up for 2 minutes, then transfer to a wire rack to cool.

When completely cold, store in an airtight container and eat within a week.

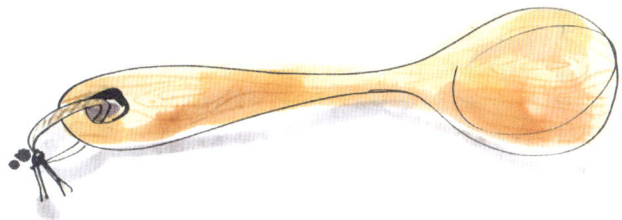

Scottish Shortbread

Butter-rich 'short' biscuits with a delicate crumbly texture have long been a speciality of Scottish bakers. The traditional recipe is simple: just fine sugar, good butter and well-sifted soft white flour in a ratio of 1 to 2 to 3 parts.

Variations abound: caster sugar is good for a sandy texture, icing sugar for a crisper 'snap'; replacing a proportion of the flour for ground rice, rice flour, cornflour, or even fine polenta, gives a lighter or less dense biscuit. Queen Victoria liked her shortbread at Balmoral made with a touch of salt to offset the sweetness. Some bakers add a pinch of caraway seeds, a dash of vanilla or almond extract, or a few finely chopped nuts. Demerara sugar is a popular addition in Dorset.

There are two methods for shortbread: either creaming soft butter with the sugar until the sugar crystals disappear and then working in the flour, or rubbing small chunks of cold butter into the flour and sugar and then gently kneading the dough together. I prefer the creaming method because the texture is finer; the sugar is fully broken down as the mixture is worked.

The mixture can be transferred to a tin for moulded biscuits, rolled out and cut into shapes, or shaped into a log and then sliced.

Petticoat Tails

These extra-buttery, thin and crisp biscuits with their distinctive shape are thought to date back to twelfth-century Edinburgh, but have been most notably associated with Mary, Queen of Scots, who had a fondness for them. Needless to say, there is some dispute among historians over both the origin of the name and the recipe. *The Cook and Housewife's Manual* (1826), written under the pseudonym Meg Dods, says, 'we rather think the name has its origins in the shape of the cakes, which is exactly that of the bell-hoop petticoats of our ancient court ladies'. The name could also derive from 'petites gatelles', old French for little cakes, or from 'tally', a historical sewing term for a cut-out pattern. The traditional design for petticoat tails is made by marking a small disc in the centre of the shaped, neatly fluted shortbread round and then cutting the surrounding dough into segments. The biscuits are finished with a dusting of caster sugar.

Makes 18 pieces

150g unsalted butter or plant butter, softened
45g icing sugar, sifted
200g plain flour
A large pinch of salt
50g cornflour
Caster sugar for sprinkling

Line two baking sheets with baking paper. Preheat the oven to 180°C.

Beat the butter until creamy using a wooden spoon or electric mixer. Scrape down the sides of the bowl, then gradually beat in the sugar, starting slowly to avoid a mess. When thoroughly combined sift the flour, salt and cornflour into the bowl and work all the ingredients together, at first using a wooden spoon, then using your hand to gently knead the mixture to make a firm dough.

Divide the dough in half and shape each piece into a neat ball. Set each in the centre of a lined baking sheet and gently press out with your hand, or a rolling pin, to an even disc 18cm across (avoid using extra flour as this can make the mixture too dry). Gently press back into shape any cracks. Pinch the outer edge of each disc to make a neat decoration, then press a 5cm plain round cutter into the centre of each disc – but do not remove the circle of dough. Using a sharp knife, cut the dough around (but not through) this circle into 8 segments.

Bake for about 18–20 minutes until lightly golden (but still pale, rather than browned) and crisp – check halfway through the baking time and rotate the baking sheets so the shortbreads bake evenly. Sprinkle with caster sugar, then gently score along the marked lines but leave on the baking sheets until completely cold.

Store in an airtight container and eat within a week.

Demerara Shortbread Rounds

Caster sugar gives this traditional recipe a sandy or short (that is, not tough) texture.

Makes 18

200g unsalted butter or plant butter, softened
100g caster sugar (golden caster works well here)
260g plain flour
35g rice flour, ground rice, cornflour or fine polenta
A large pinch of salt
About 35g demerara sugar for coating

Beat the butter until creamy using a wooden spoon or electric mixer. Beat in the sugar until the mixture is lighter in colour and fluffy. Sift the flour, rice flour (or ground rice, cornflour or polenta) and salt into the bowl and work all the ingredients together, at first using a wooden spoon, then using your hand to gently knead the mixture to make a firm dough.

Form the dough into a neat log 5cm across and 18cm long. Scatter the demerara sugar over a large sheet of baking paper and roll the log back and forth in the sugar until evenly coated, then wrap tightly in the paper and chill for 15 minutes.

Meanwhile, preheat the oven to 180°C and line two baking sheets with baking paper.

Unwrap the log and cut into 18 slices using a large sharp knife. Arrange slightly apart on the lined sheets, then bake for about 15–18 minutes until firm and pale golden. Leave to firm up for 3–4 minutes, then transfer to a wire rack to cool.

When completely cold, store in an airtight container and eat within a week.

Vanilla or Lavender Rounds

Flavour the mixture with ¼–½ teaspoon vanilla extract (to taste), adding it with the caster sugar. Alternatively, rub a large pinch of culinary lavender with the sugar to release the oils and scents, then add to the butter and finish the recipe as given on facing page.

Ginger Shortbread

Add ½ teaspoon ground ginger and 50g chopped glacé ginger along with the flour; finish the recipe as given on facing page.

Speckled Shortbread

Chill 50g dark chocolate (about 70 per cent cocoa solids). Make the dough as in the main recipe and form into a log, but omit the demerara coating. Cut into slices and arrange the rounds slightly apart on the lined baking sheets. Grate the cold chocolate and carefully scatter over the tops of the shortbreads, then bake as given on facing page.

Pistachio Shortbread

Add 50g unsalted pistachio kernels, chopped medium-fine, to the dough when you work in the flour. If you like you can blanch the nuts (see page 116) for a brighter colour. Shape the dough into a log, omit the demerara coating, then slice and bake as given on facing page.

Chocolate Shortbread Fingers

Replace the rice flour with cocoa powder. Press the dough into a greased and base-lined 20cm square tin to form an even layer (use your fingers or the back of a spoon). Prick the dough well with a fork, then score into 18 fingers with the tip of a sharp knife. Bake for about 18–20 minutes until firm but not too dark. Put the tin on a wire rack and score along the marked lines. Sprinkle with caster sugar, but leave until cold before removing from the tin.

Chapter 2
All About Chocolate

Chocolate Chip Cookies

The classic, irregular-looking cookie is usually made with chunks of good chocolate – either chocolate baking chips or a chopped-up dark chocolate bar – along with crunchy pieces of walnuts or pecans.

Here are three recipes: one with cocoa powder to pack a real punch; a vanilla cookie with a buttery, short texture; and a fun, nut-free version, decorated with Smarties. They are quite high in sugar and, depending on your oven and its hot spots, can colour quickly.

Double Chocolate Chip Cookies

Makes about 24

125g unsalted butter, softened
100g light muscovado sugar
100g caster sugar
1 medium egg, beaten
220g plain flour
A large pinch of salt
½ tsp baking powder

½ tsp bicarbonate of soda
20g cocoa powder
100g dark chocolate baking chips
   or chopped dark chocolate
   (about 70 per cent cocoa solids)
100g pecan or walnut pieces

Line two baking sheets with baking paper. Preheat the oven to 180°C.

Beat the butter with both sugars until soft and fluffy, then gradually beat in the egg. Sift in the flour, salt, baking powder, bicarbonate of soda and cocoa powder and mix in with a wooden spoon. Add the chocolate chips or chunks and the nuts and mix until thoroughly combined into a firm dough.

Scoop up the dough and roll between your hands to make walnut-sized balls. Arrange well apart on the baking sheets to allow for spreading, then gently flatten slightly. Bake for about 15 minutes until just firm – rotate the baking sheets after 10 minutes for even baking. Leave to firm up for about 5 minutes, then transfer to a wire rack to cool.

When completely cold, store in an airtight container and eat within a week.

Chocolate Chip Vanilla Cookies

Makes about 20

125g unsalted butter, softened
50g light muscovado sugar
50g caster sugar
½ tsp vanilla extract
1 medium egg, beaten
150g plain flour
½ tsp baking powder
100g dark chocolate baking chips or chopped dark chocolate (about 70 per cent cocoa solids)
50g walnut pieces
¼ tsp sea salt flakes

Line two baking sheets with baking paper. Preheat the oven to 190°C.

Beat the butter with both sugars until creamy and lighter in texture. Beat in the vanilla, then gradually beat in the egg.

Sift the flour and baking powder into the bowl and mix in with a wooden spoon or rubber spatula to make a firm dough. Add the chocolate and nuts and work in. When thoroughly combined, sprinkle the salt over the dough and gently work in.

Scoop up a heaped teaspoon of the dough and use another teaspoon to push the dough onto the baking sheets, making small irregular mounds and spacing them well apart. Bake for about 9–12 minutes until the cookies are just firm and lightly golden with darker edges – rotate the baking sheets after 6 minutes for even baking. Leave to firm up for a couple of minutes, then transfer to a wire rack to cool.

When completely cold, store in an airtight container and eat within a week.

Party Cookies

Makes 12

125g unsalted butter, softened
100g light muscovado sugar
50g caster sugar
½ tsp vanilla extract
1 medium egg, beaten
130g plain flour, plus extra for dusting

¼ tsp salt
½ tsp baking powder
90g porridge oats
85g chocolate chips of your choice
60 Smarties (about 2 tubes) to decorate

Line two baking sheets with baking paper. Preheat the oven to 180°C.

Beat the butter with both sugars and the vanilla in a large mixing bowl until light and fluffy. Scrape down the sides of the bowl, then beat in the egg, beating well for a couple of minutes, then scrape down the sides of the bowl again. Add the flour, salt, baking powder, oats and chocolate chips; mix with a wooden spoon until thoroughly combined and the choc chips are evenly distributed.

Divide the mixture into 12, then lightly flour your hands and roll each portion into a ball. Arrange well apart on the baking sheets and gently flatten to make discs about 1cm thick and 7cm across. Press five Smarties on top of each.

Bake for about 15–16 minutes or until just firm and golden with slightly darker edges – rotate the baking sheets after 10 minutes for even baking. Leave to firm up for a couple of minutes, then transfer to a wire rack to cool.

When completely cold, store in an airtight container and eat within a week.

Dark Chocolate Crackles

These delicious cookies have a distinctive 'crazy paving' appearance thanks to the addition of bicarbonate of soda: this helps the dough expand in the heat of the oven; it then deflates on cooling.

It is important to use the right dark chocolate here for a good melt-in-the-mouth texture and flavour: a bar with 70 per cent cocoa solids is fine, a much higher percentage will make the biscuits a bit dry, while much lower will lack the perfect cocoa 'hit'.

By the way, these are the best biscuits to use with vanilla ice cream for ice-cream sandwiches.

Makes about 20

100g dark chocolate (about 70 per cent cocoa solids)
100g unsalted butter, very soft
150g light muscovado sugar
1 medium egg, at room temperature
½ tsp vanilla extract
175g self-raising flour
½ tsp bicarbonate of soda
¼ tsp sea salt flakes
2–3 tbsp icing sugar

Break or chop the chocolate into even-sized pieces about the size of your thumbnail and put into a heatproof bowl large enough to hold all the ingredients. Set over a pan of steaming hot water and leave to melt gently. Alternatively, melt the chocolate in the microwave (see page 10).

Remove the bowl from the pan and stir in the butter, a little at a time. When completely incorporated and smooth, stir in the sugar.

Using a fork, beat the egg with the vanilla. Check the chocolate mixture is barely warm (if not, leave for a couple of minutes), then beat the egg into the chocolate mixture using a wooden spoon.

Sift the flour and bicarbonate of soda into the bowl and mix in, then add the salt flakes and mix until thoroughly combined. Cover the bowl and chill for 20 minutes.

Meanwhile, preheat the oven to 200°C and line two baking sheets with baking paper.

Using a tablespoon measure, scoop out the dough and roll into walnut-sized balls. Sift the icing sugar into a shallow bowl and roll each ball in the sugar to give a good coating.

Set the balls on the lined baking sheets, spacing them well apart to allow for spreading. Bake for 11 minutes for a soft-centred biscuit, or a couple of minutes more for a crisper one; they will continue to cook for a few minutes after they come out of the oven.

Leave to firm up for a few minutes, then transfer to a wire rack to cool.

When completely cold, store in an airtight container and eat within a week.

Double Chocolate Twists

Made from twisted ropes of dark- and white-chocolate studded dough, these are distinctly rich and crumbly. It is wise to chill the twists before they go into the oven so that they keep a good shape.

Makes 24

125g unsalted butter, softened
85g caster sugar
1 medium egg, at room temperature
½ tsp vanilla extract
225g plain flour
¼ tsp salt
10g cornflour
50g white chocolate (at least 30 per cent cocoa butter)
50g dark chocolate (70–80 per cent cocoa solids)

To finish

1 tbsp cocoa nibs, pearl sugar or chocolate sprinkles (all optional) for sprinkling
Icing sugar for dusting

Line two baking sheets with baking paper.

Beat the butter and sugar together until creamy using a wooden spoon or electric mixer. Using a fork, beat the egg with the vanilla, then beat into the butter mixture in three additions, beating well after each addition.

Scrape down the sides of the bowl, then sift the flour, salt and cornflour onto the mixture. Work in using a wooden spoon at first, then using your hand to bring the mixture together to form a ball of dough. Divide the dough in half and transfer one half to another bowl.

Grate or very finely chop the white chocolate and add to one bowl, then mix in with a wooden spoon. Gently knead the dough in the bowl – you don't want to melt the chocolate – then turn it out onto an unfloured worktop. Divide the dough into 4 equal pieces and use your hands to roll each one into a neat sausage 1cm thick and 40cm long. Move them to one side of the worktop. Repeat this stage using the second portion of dough and the dark chocolate.

Lay a white chocolate sausage next to a dark chocolate one, then gently twist them together. If the dough breaks, gently press it back into shape. Trim each end of the dough rope, then cut it into 6 equal lengths. Repeat with the remaining dough sausages to make 24 pieces in total.

Arrange the twists well apart on the lined baking sheets, then sprinkle with the cocoa nibs, pearl sugar or chocolate sprinkles, if using. Chill for 30 minutes.

Towards the end of this time, preheat the oven to 190°C.

Bake the twists for 11–15 minutes until barely golden and firm. Leave to firm up on the baking sheets for 5 minutes, then transfer to a wire rack to cool.

When completely cold, dust with icing sugar. Store in an airtight container and eat within 5 days.

French Chocolate Fingers

These elegant, rich, melt-in-the-mouth biscuits are piped to form ridged fingers. After baking they are finished with dashes of melted chocolate.

Makes 20

175g unsalted butter or plant butter, softened
50g caster sugar
½ tsp vanilla extract
25g cocoa powder
150g plain flour
A large pinch of salt
¼ tsp baking powder

To finish

75g good-quality white, milk or dark chocolate (vegan if preferred)

Line two baking sheets with baking paper.

Using an electric mixer or wooden spoon, beat the butter until creamy, with the texture of mayonnaise. Add the sugar and vanilla and beat until the mixture is light and fluffy. Sift the cocoa powder, flour, salt and baking powder into the bowl and fold in using a rubber spatula or metal spoon until thoroughly combined.

Transfer the mixture to a piping bag fitted with a large star tube. Pipe the mixture onto the lined baking sheets in fingers 9cm long, spacing them well apart to allow for spreading. Chill for 30 minutes.

Towards the end of this time, preheat the oven to 180°C.

Bake the fingers for about 13–15 minutes until slightly darker around the edges. Leave on the baking sheets until completely cold before transferring to a wire rack as they are very fragile.

To finish, break or chop the chocolate into even-sized pieces and put into a heatproof bowl. Melt gently, either over a pan of steaming water or in the microwave (see page 10). Stir until smooth, then dip a fork into the melted chocolate and flick it backwards and forwards over the fingers. It's a good idea to line the worktop with baking paper first to avoid any mess.

Leave until completely set before serving or storing in an airtight container. Best eaten within 5 days.

Chocolate Oaties

For this quick and easy recipe everything is simply mixed in a saucepan, then scooped onto a baking sheet in small mounds and popped in the oven. It's very adaptable, so use the chocolate and nuts you prefer: milk, white or dark chocolate drops, or a chopped-up bar, plus walnut or pecan pieces, roughly chopped hazelnuts, pistachios, almonds or cashews, or a mixture.

Makes about 24

125g unsalted butter
100g light muscovado sugar
100g caster sugar
1 medium egg
½ tsp vanilla extract
150g porridge oats
125g plain flour

¼ tsp salt
¼ tsp bicarbonate of soda
50g good-quality chocolate – milk, white or dark (or a mix), baking drops or bar
50g nuts – pieces or roughly chopped

Line two baking sheets with baking paper. Preheat the oven to 180°C.

Put the butter and both sugars into a saucepan large enough to hold all the ingredients. Set over a low heat until the butter has melted. Remove from the heat and stir with a wooden spoon until smooth. Set aside to cool.

Meanwhile, using a fork, beat the egg with the vanilla. Mix the oats with the flour, salt and bicarbonate of soda. If necessary, chop the chocolate into pieces the size of your little fingernail, then combine the chocolate and the nuts.

Add the egg mixture to the pan and beat well for a minute or so with the wooden spoon, then stir in the oat mixture. The mixture should be just warm, though not hot, or it will be difficult to work in the oat mix. Add the chocolate and nuts and stir until evenly distributed.

Using a tablespoon measure, scoop the dough onto the lined baking sheets in small heaps, spacing them well apart to allow for spreading. Bake for about 15–17 minutes until lightly golden. Leave to firm up on the baking sheets for about 5 minutes, then transfer to a wire rack to cool (the chocolate will still be warm, so take care).

When completely cold, store in an airtight container and eat within a week.

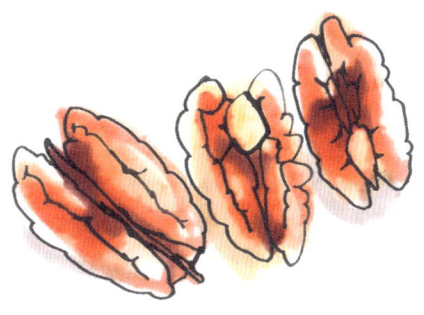

The National Trust's Double Choc, Pistachio and Sea Salt Cookies (GF)

The National Trust's chefs devised this deliciously rich recipe to use up those uneaten or broken Easter eggs – though of course you can use any good chocolate at any time of the year. It uses buckwheat flour, a gluten-free flour with plenty of flavour, rather than wheat flour. The dark cookies are finished with jewel-bright pistachios and a sprinkling of sea salt flakes.

Makes 12

150g good chocolate – milk chocolate with a high percentage of cocoa solids, or 70 per cent dark chocolate, or a combination
35g unsalted butter, very soft
60g light muscovado sugar
¼ tsp vanilla extract
1 medium egg, beaten

85g buckwheat flour
15g cocoa powder
¼ tsp bicarbonate of soda
A large pinch of salt
15g pistachio kernels, lightly crushed
Sea salt flakes for sprinkling

Line two baking sheets with baking paper. Preheat the oven to 180°C.

Chop or break the chocolate into even-sized pieces about the size of your little fingernail. Set half the pieces aside and put the rest into a heatproof bowl. Melt gently, either over a pan of steaming water or in the microwave (see page 10), stir until smooth, then set aside.

Beat the butter and sugar together using a wooden spoon or electric mixer, then beat in the vanilla, the egg and the cooled but still fluid chocolate. Mix until thoroughly combined.

Sift the flour, cocoa powder, bicarbonate of soda and salt into the bowl. Add the reserved chocolate pieces and mix everything together with a wooden spoon or rubber spatula to make a very stiff dough.

Using your hands, roll the mixture into 12 walnut-sized balls and set them well apart on the lined sheets. Gently flatten each ball to about 1cm thick. Scatter the pistachios over the cookies.

Bake for about 11–12 minutes until barely firm (take care not to touch the molten chocolate). For good, moist chocolate cookies avoid overbaking – watch them carefully: they will continue to cook for a few minutes after they come out of the oven.

Remove from the oven and sprinkle lightly with sea salt flakes. Leave to firm up for a few minutes, then transfer to a wire rack to cool.

When completely cold, store in an airtight container and eat within 5 days.

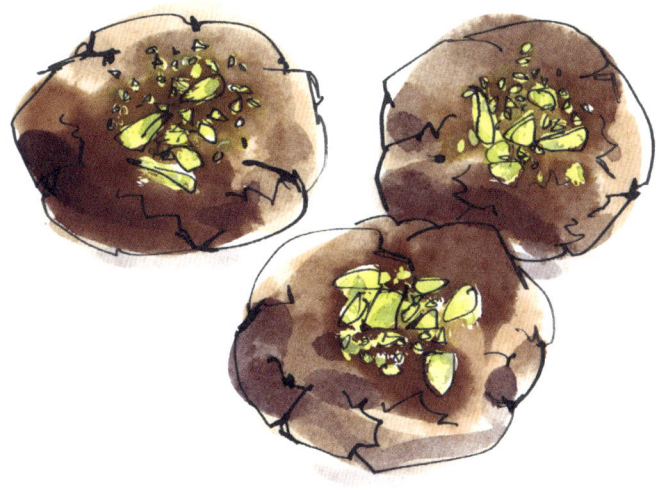

Walnut Chocolate Crumbles

Melted chocolate, quickly piped or drizzled, adds the final touch to buttery, crisp biscuits studded with toasted walnuts. You could also use hazelnuts, pecans or almonds or a mix of nuts, or use two different types of chocolate for even fancier biscuits.

Makes 16

100g walnut pieces
100g unsalted butter, softened
100g caster sugar
40g demerara sugar
1 medium egg, at room temperature
½ tsp vanilla extract

250g self-raising flour, plus extra for dusting
¼ tsp salt

To finish

75g good-quality chocolate – dark, milk or white (or a mix)

Line two baking sheets with baking paper. Preheat the oven to 180°C.

If necessary, chop the nuts slightly smaller so they are about pea-sized. Set 15g aside. Tip the remaining 85g into an ovenproof dish and toast in the oven for about 6–8 minutes until golden. Set aside to cool.

Put the butter and both sugars into a mixing bowl and beat well using a wooden spoon or electric mixer. Using a fork, beat the egg with the vanilla, then beat into the butter and sugar mixture until thoroughly combined.

Sift the flour and salt into the bowl and work in with a wooden spoon or rubber spatula. When the mixture starts to come together, tip the cooled toasted walnuts into the bowl and gently knead the dough, using your hands to bring it together.

Lightly flour your hands and roll the dough into 16 walnut-sized balls. Set them well apart on the lined baking sheets, then gently flatten them so each biscuit is about 1.25cm thick. Scatter the reserved nuts over the biscuits and gently press them onto the dough.

Bake for about 14–16 minutes until the biscuits are golden with light brown edges – check after 10 minutes and rotate the baking sheets if necessary so they cook evenly. Remove from the oven and leave until cold.

To finish, chop or break the chocolate into even-sized pieces and put into a heatproof bowl. Melt gently, either over a pan of steaming water or in the microwave (see page 10). Stir gently until the chocolate is smooth. Spoon it into a small piping bag, or a small plastic bag and snip off the tip, then pipe zigzag lines over each biscuit. Alternatively, dip a fork or teaspoon into the melted chocolate and drizzle or swirl it over. For a striped finish, use two different chocolates: add the darker one first and leave it to set before adding the second decoration.

Once the chocolate has set, store in an airtight container and eat within 5 days.

White Chocolate, Sour Cherry and Pistachio Cookies

Soft-dried dark red sour or morello cherries have a delicious sharpness that works well with good-quality white chocolate, and vivid green pistachios add texture. These small, elegant cookies are ideal with an after-dinner coffee.

Makes about 24

125g unsalted butter, very soft but not runny
100g light muscovado sugar
1 medium egg
½ tsp vanilla extract
165g plain flour
½ tsp baking powder
A large pinch of salt
90g good white chocolate (at least 30 per cent cocoa butter), chopped into pea-sized chunks
50g soft-dried sour cherries
25g pistachio kernels, halved

Line two baking sheets with baking paper. Preheat the oven to 180°C.

Put the butter, sugar, egg and vanilla into a mixing bowl. Sift the flour, baking powder and salt into the bowl and beat with a wooden spoon or electric mixer until thoroughly combined.

Add the chocolate, cherries and pistachios to the bowl and mix in with a wooden spoon until evenly distributed.

Scoop up a heaped teaspoon of the mixture and use another teaspoon to push the mixture onto the baking sheets in rough mounds, spacing them well apart to allow for spreading.

Bake for about 15 minutes until firm and a light golden colour with darker edges. Leave to firm up on the baking sheets for a couple of minutes, then transfer to a wire rack to cool.

When completely cold, store in an airtight container and eat within a week.

The Richest Chocolate Biscuits

The principal ingredient is dark chocolate, melted and made into a mixture like a baked mousse, with added chocolate chips. Chilling the dough before shaping and baking gives a neat result.

For a quick dessert, sandwich together with a scoop of vanilla ice cream.

Makes 24

125g dark chocolate (about 70 per cent cocoa solids), chopped
20g unsalted butter, diced
Scant ½ tsp instant coffee granules or powder
½ tsp boiling water
1 medium egg, at room temperature
75g caster sugar
25g plain flour
¼ tsp baking powder
100g chocolate chips or drops (milk chocolate with around 40 per cent cocoa solids, or dark chocolate with around 70 per cent cocoa solids)
¼ tsp sea salt flakes

Put the chopped chocolate into a heatproof bowl with the butter and set over a pan of steaming hot water (don't let the base of the bowl touch the water); leave to melt gently. Stir briefly, then remove from the pan and set aside.

Put the coffee into a mixing bowl or the bowl of an electric mixer; if using granules, crush to a powder with the back of a spoon. Add ½ teaspoon boiling water and stir until dissolved. Add the egg and sugar to the bowl and whisk on high speed with an electric whisk for about 3 minutes until the mixture is thick and mousse-like.

Using the slowest speed, whisk in the melted chocolate. Sift the flour and baking powder onto the mixture and fold in using a rubber spatula or large metal spoon. Scatter over the choc chips and the sea salt flakes and fold in until evenly distributed.

Turn out the mixture onto a large sheet of baking paper and form into a log 5cm across and 24cm long, using your hands and the paper to help you. Wrap and chill for 30 minutes until firm enough to slice easily.

Towards the end of this time, preheat the oven to 180°C and line two baking sheets with baking paper.

Using a large sharp knife, cut the log into 24 slices, pushing back into place any stray choc chips. Arrange the slices well apart on the lined baking sheets and bake for about 14–16 minutes until the biscuits have a craggy, cracked look, are just firm and have slightly darker edges. Leave to firm up on the baking sheets for about 5 minutes, then transfer to a wire rack to cool.

When completely cold, store in an airtight container and eat within 5 days.

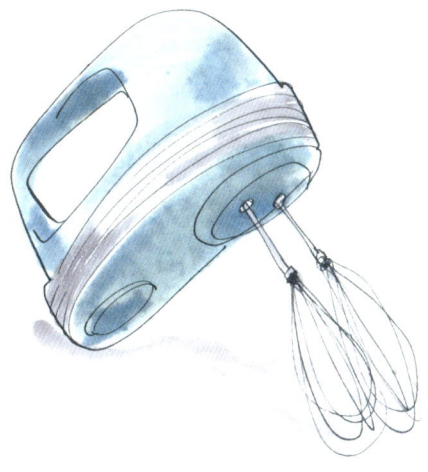

White Chocolate, Pine Nut and Chilli Cookies

A recipe from Sante Fe, New Mexico, where the piñon is the much-prized nut of the official state tree and where, according to archaeological evidence, people were using cocoa beans at least 1,000 years ago. Chilli, cinnamon or vanilla are the usual additions to chocolate drinks, as well as to ice creams and confectionery.

This recipe includes Tabasco, a hot chilli pepper sauce. Add just a few drops for a mild 'mystery ingredient' flavour, more if you like a warm kick.

Makes about 24

130g pine nuts
200g plain flour
½ tsp baking powder
A large pinch of salt
110g light muscovado sugar
115g unsalted butter, very soft but not runny

1 medium egg
½ tsp vanilla extract
5 drops Tabasco, or to taste
100g good white chocolate (at least 30 per cent cocoa butter), chopped into chunks

---

Line two baking sheets with baking paper. Preheat the oven to 180°C.

Put the nuts into an ovenproof dish and toast in the oven for about 5 minutes until a light golden colour – watch carefully as they quickly burn. Leave to cool.

Meanwhile, sift the flour, baking powder, salt and sugar into a mixing bowl. Add the butter.

Using a fork, beat the egg in a small bowl with the vanilla and Tabasco – carefully add 5 drops for a mild flavour, or ¼ teaspoon for more of a kick, or even more if liked! – until combined, then add to the bowl along with the chocolate chunks and the nuts; mix well with a wooden spoon until the ingredients are thoroughly combined.

Using a tablespoon measure, scoop out a tablespoon of the dough and drop it onto the lined baking sheet. Repeat with the remaining dough, spacing the cookies well apart to allow for spreading.

Bake for about 12–15 minutes until a light golden colour with darker edges. Leave to firm up for a couple of minutes, then transfer the cookies to a wire rack to cool.

When completely cold, store in an airtight container and eat within 5 days.

Chapter 3
Something Fancy

Florentines

These pretty, slightly chewy confections are made with nuts and fruit, then finished with a coating of chocolate on the base. Two types of nuts and two of fruit provide contrasts in colour, texture and flavour. Almonds are often used, along with pistachios, walnut pieces, hazelnuts or Kent cobnuts for crunch. Red glacé cherries are traditional, but the darker soft-dried sour cherries are an excellent counterbalance to the sweetness. Sultanas, crystallised or candied fruits or peel are the most common additions.

Makes about 14

60g blanched almonds
45g soft-dried sour cherries or glacé cherries
20g pistachios, walnut pieces, hazelnuts or cobnuts
40g sultanas or crystallised fruit or peel (or a mix)
15g plain flour
A large pinch of salt

45g unsalted butter or plant butter
60g demerara sugar
1 tbsp double cream or non-dairy cream

To finish

125g dark chocolate (about 70 per cent cocoa solids, vegan if preferred)

Line two baking sheets with baking paper. Preheat the oven to 180°C.

Roughly chop the almonds or cut into slivers; halve dried cherries, or quarter glacé cherries; roughly chop pistachios, walnut pieces, hazelnuts or cobnuts; if using crystallised fruit or peel, chop into pieces about the same size as the cherries. Put all the nuts and fruit – including the sultanas, if using – into a bowl.

Sift the flour and salt onto a sheet of baking paper.

Put the butter and sugar into a saucepan large enough to hold all the ingredients, set over a low heat and melt gently, stirring until smooth. Remove the pan from the heat and stir in the cream, followed by the fruit and nut mixture, then the sifted flour and salt. Mix well until all the ingredients are evenly distributed.

Scoop up a heaped teaspoon of the mixture and drop it onto a lined baking sheet. Gently flatten the middle – the mixture will spread out in the oven. Repeat with the remaining mixture, spacing the Florentines well apart.

Bake for about 10–12 minutes until a good golden brown – watch them carefully and rotate the sheets after 6 minutes so they bake evenly. Leave to firm up for about 5 minutes, then carefully transfer to a wire rack to cool – the biscuits will be very fragile.

When the Florentines are completely cold, chop or break the chocolate into even-sized pieces, put in a heatproof bowl and melt gently, either over a pan of steaming water or in the microwave (see page 10). Remove the bowl from the heat and spread a fine, even layer of chocolate on the flat underside of each Florentine. Leave to set, chocolate side up, on a sheet of baking paper; just before it starts to set, use a fork to make a wavy pattern in the chocolate.

Leave until completely set, then store in an airtight container and eat within 4 days.

Gingerbread People

Although gingerbread shapes were sold at fairs during the medieval period, gingerbread men or, more specifically, figures of Guy Fawkes, became popular following the discovery of the Gunpowder Plot in 1605, and Bonfire Night celebrations continue to include gingerbread to this day.

The spicy dark gingerbread dough is easy to make, roll out and cut into shapes: you can find cutters in the shape of people, stars, bells or even dinosaurs. These shapes can be decorated with dried fruit, nuts or chocolate drops pressed into the dough before baking, or with a simple homemade glacé icing or ready-made writing icing when cold.

Makes about 20 x 12cm figures or shapes

350g plain flour, plus extra for dusting
4 tsp ground ginger
1 tsp ground cinnamon
½ tsp ground mixed spice
A large pinch of salt
1 tsp bicarbonate of soda
170g dark muscovado sugar
125g unsalted butter, chilled and diced

85g golden syrup
1 medium egg, at room temperature
Dried fruit, nuts, chocolate drops, or hundreds and thousands to decorate

For the glacé icing (optional)

100g icing sugar
3–4 tsp lemon juice
Edible food colouring

To make the dough in a food processor: tip the flour into the processor bowl, then add the ginger, cinnamon, mixed spice, salt, bicarbonate of soda and the sugar. Pulse a few times until thoroughly combined and lump-free. Add the butter and process to make fine crumbs. Weigh the golden syrup into a small bowl, add the egg and beat with a fork, then add to the processor and pulse until the mixture comes together to make a dough.

To make in a mixing bowl: sift all the dry ingredients (including the sugar) into a large bowl, then add the pieces of butter and rub into the flour mixture using the tips of your fingers (or cut in with a metal pastry blender), until the mixture looks like fine crumbs. Weigh the golden syrup into a small bowl, add the egg and beat with a fork, then add to the mixing bowl and work into the flour mixture using a wooden spoon. Use your hands to shape the dough into a ball.

Turn out the dough onto a lightly floured worktop and knead it gently for a couple of seconds, then shape it into a thick, flat disc. Wrap the dough and chill for 15 minutes.

Meanwhile, preheat the oven to 180°C and line two baking sheets with baking paper.

Lightly dust the worktop and your cutters with flour, then unwrap the dough and roll it out to about the thickness of a pound coin. Stamp out shapes and set them well apart on the lined sheets to allow for spreading. Gather up the trimmings, gently knead them together, then roll out again and cut more shapes. Decorate with dried fruit, nuts or chocolate drops for features, buttons and hair – any iced features are added later.

Bake for 11–15 minutes until a rich golden brown with slightly darker edges. Leave to firm up for about 5 minutes, then transfer to a wire rack to cool. Leave until completely cold before decorating with icing.

To make glacé icing: sift the icing sugar into a small bowl, then gradually stir in enough lemon juice to make a smooth icing that holds its shape for piping. Leave white or add a little edible colouring – a drop on the end of a cocktail stick may be enough. Transfer to a ready-made piping bag, or, if you don't have a piping bag, make a bag from baking paper, or use a small plastic bag with the very tip of one corner cut off. Pipe features, hair, clothes, names or just squiggles, then add any sugar decorations like hundreds and thousands, if using, and leave to set.

Store in an airtight container and eat within 5 days.

Brandy Snaps

Delicate, crisp and slightly spicy, these are the most glamorous biscuits to enjoy with coffee or a creamy dessert. They are simply made in a saucepan, but the baking and shaping are time-sensitive and need a bit of care.

Makes about 24

85g unsalted butter or plant butter
85g caster sugar
65g golden syrup
85g plain flour

A pinch of salt
1 tsp ground ginger
2 tsp brandy

Line two baking sheets with baking paper. Preheat the oven to 180°C.

Weigh the butter, sugar and golden syrup into a small saucepan. Sift the flour, salt and ginger onto a sheet of baking paper.

Set the saucepan over a low heat and stir with a wooden spoon until the mixture is melted and smooth. Remove the pan from the heat and tip in the flour mixture, add the brandy and mix well to make a smooth, thick batter.

Using a heaped teaspoon of batter for each biscuit, drop the mixture onto the lined baking sheets, spacing them about 10cm apart to allow for spreading – there is no need to spread out the mixture. Start by baking just two biscuits to test the baking time and practice the shaping: bake for about 7–10 minutes until the biscuits are chestnut brown – watch carefully. Remove the baking sheet from the oven, leave to cool for exactly 1 minute, then carefully lift off one biscuit using a palette knife and quickly roll and mould it around a thick spoon handle to make a hollow roll.

The mixture will rapidly firm up so you need to be speedy. If the mixture hardens before it can be shaped, return the baking sheet to the oven for a minute until pliable again. Leave the rolls to cool on the spoon handle until set, then gently slide off and place on a wire rack. Once you have the timings worked out you can bake in batches of three or four.

Store in an airtight container and eat within 4 days.

Chocolate-dipped Brandy Snaps

Melt 75g dark chocolate (see page 10) in a small deep bowl, then dip each end of the cooled, rolled Brandy Snaps in the melted chocolate and leave to set on a sheet of baking paper.

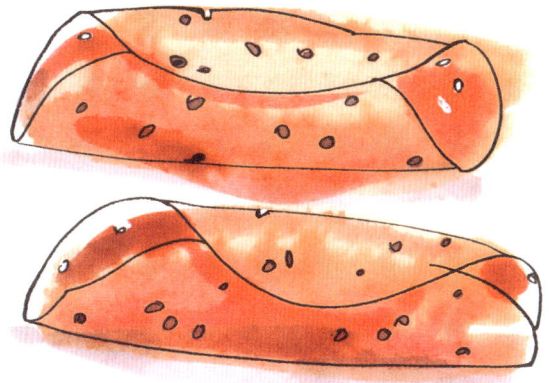

Lebkuchen

An essential part of Christmas in Germany, lebkuchen are made in almost any shape and size, plain or glazed, or moulded and heavily decorated. Originally baked by monks in Nuremburg in 1395, the traditional recipe consists of honey and seven spices to represent the seven days of the Creation, as told in the Bible. By the sixteenth century the town – situated on a network of roads leading across Europe – had become wealthy as a centre of the exotic luxury spice trade, and was also renowned for fine honey and nuts, all key ingredients for lebkuchen. Nuremburg later became known for chocolate, too.

For centuries, only master guildsmen were authorised to bake and sell the sweet and tongue-tinglingly spicy lebkuchen in the annual Advent market, but today there are many versions and bakers.

This recipe has a long list of ingredients but is simple to put together; right after baking the hot lebkuchen are finished with a shiny white glacé icing and a dark chocolate one.

Note: keep the lebkuchen for a day or so after baking, for the spices and honey to develop a deep, complex flavour and texture.

Makes about 26

225g clear honey
45g dark muscovado sugar
85g unsalted butter
Finely grated zest of 1 orange
Finely grated zest of 1 unwaxed lemon, plus 1 tbsp juice
50g chopped glacé ginger or drained stem ginger
250g plain flour
85g ground almonds
1 tsp baking powder
½ tsp bicarbonate of soda
A large pinch of salt
2 tsp ground ginger
1 tsp ground cinnamon
¼ tsp grated nutmeg
¼ tsp ground cloves
½ tsp ground mixed spice
3 grinds of black pepper
Seeds from 2 cardamom pods, finely ground

To glaze

50g icing sugar
1 medium egg white, at room temperature
50g dark chocolate (about 70 per cent cocoa solids)
15g unsalted butter, at room temperature

Weigh the honey, sugar and butter into a saucepan. Add the orange and lemon zests and the lemon juice. Chop the ginger very finely and add to the pan, then set it over a low heat and leave the mixture to melt gently, stirring frequently.

Sift the flour, ground almonds, baking powder, bicarbonate of soda, salt, and all the spices into a large mixing bowl and make a well in the centre. Pour the melted mixture into the well and gradually work in the dry ingredients using a wooden spoon to make a heavy, sticky dough. Cover and leave in a cool place to firm up for about an hour (or about 30 minutes in the fridge).

When ready to bake, line two baking sheets with baking paper and preheat the oven to 180°C.

Using a tablespoon measure, scoop up a tablespoon of the mixture and roll it between your hands to a neat ball. Place it on a lined baking sheet and gently flatten so it is 1cm thick and 5cm across. Repeat with the remaining mixture, spacing the balls well apart to allow for spreading.

Bake for 12–15 minutes or until just firm when pressed very gently in the centre – check after 10 minutes and rotate the sheets so the biscuits bake evenly.

Meanwhile, make the glazes so they are ready when the biscuits emerge. Sift the icing sugar into a small bowl. In another small bowl, beat the egg white with a fork until frothy. Gradually stir enough egg white (about 3–4 teaspoons) into the sugar to make a smooth icing with the consistency of thin cream. To make the dark chocolate glaze: finely chop the chocolate and put it into a heatproof bowl with the butter and 1 tablespoon water. Set over a pan of steaming hot water and leave to melt. Remove the bowl from the heat and stir briefly and gently to make a thick, smooth glaze.

A soon as the biscuits are ready, remove the baking sheets from the oven and set on a heatproof surface. Using a pastry brush, quickly brush the icing sugar glaze over half of each biscuit. Leave on the baking sheets for 5 minutes to cool slightly, then using an offset palette knife or round-bladed knife quickly spread the chocolate glaze over the other (unglazed) half of each still-warm biscuit. Leave to set until completely cold.

Store in an airtight container for a day or two before eating. Best eaten within a week.

Macaroons (GF)

There seems to be no end of types of macaroons or *macarons* around today; it's a wide-ranging family – not surprising given its distant origins. Some food historians have traced these kinds of small cakes of finely ground nuts, sugar and egg whites back to AD 791 and a monastery in the Loire region of France, though similar confections, flavoured with citrus, seem to have appeared all over Europe around that time, having come from Persia via North Africa to Spain and Sicily.

In the Middle Ages, Siena in central Italy was an important commercial and cultural centre; its small, tender, oval ricciarelli biscuits were much appreciated. The recipe sounds similar to one quoted in Jill Norman's book *The English Table*: a recipe for 'English Macaroons' appeared in *The Italian Confectioner* (published in 1823); it called for 'one pound of sweet almonds, one pound and a quarter of sugar, six whites of eggs, and the raspings of two lemons.' They were baked in oval shapes on wafer paper.

In Britain a much-loved staple of cake shops and tea-rooms has long been a round, slightly domed, crisp confection with a sticky centre, made with ground almonds, sugar and egg whites, decorated with whole or flaked almonds, and traditionally baked on rice paper: this is the macaroon. The recipe hasn't changed much since it first appeared in print in 1617, though the gooey mixture was then baked on wafers and served with small glasses of sweet wine. James Boswell, the diarist and biographer of Samuel Johnson, wrote of eating almond biscuits, known as macaroons, in London in the late eighteenth century.

In the late nineteenth century, bakers in the United States adapted a flourless recipe, using less expensive desiccated coconut instead of almonds. A deliciously rich version with a chocolate base is especially popular during Passover.

Elegant, glossy and chic French *macarons* as we know them today first appeared in Paris; they are now baked in every possible colour and flavour and sandwiched in pairs with a ganache or a sweet buttercream filling.

To quote novelist Henry James: 'A tradition is kept alive only by something being added to it.' Here are four interesting variations on the macaroon.

Note: the flavour and texture of all the macaroons develop and are best a day or so after baking.

Macaroons – British Tea-room Style

Makes about 12

125g ground almonds
175g caster sugar
10g cornflour
2 medium egg whites, at room temperature

A pinch of salt
½ tsp almond extract
1 tbsp flaked almonds to decorate

Line two baking sheets with baking paper. Preheat the oven to 160°C.

Sift the ground almonds, sugar and cornflour into a mixing bowl. Put the egg whites into another bowl, add the salt and whisk with a fork until frothy, then mix in the almond extract. Add this to the ground almond mixture and mix everything together with a wooden spoon to make a stiff dough.

Scoop out the mixture using a tablespoon measure for each macaroon, spacing the mounds well apart on the lined baking sheets. Gently spread out each mound to form a disc about 1.5cm high and 5cm across (they will expand in the oven). Scatter some flaked almonds over the top of each disc.

Bake for about 20–25 minutes until golden. Leave to firm up for about 10 minutes, then transfer to a wire rack to cool.

When completely cold, store in an airtight container and eat within a week.

Ricciarelli – Oval Soft-Style Macaroons from Siena

Note: this dough needs to be chilled for several hours before baking.

Makes 25

250g ground almonds
200g icing sugar, plus extra for dusting
¼ tsp baking powder
2 medium egg whites, at room temperature

A large pinch of salt
½ tsp almond extract
Finely grated zest of ½ unwaxed orange

Sift the ground almonds, icing sugar and baking powder into a mixing bowl; set aside.

Put the egg whites and salt into a large, spotlessly clean, grease-free mixing bowl and whisk using an electric mixer until the whites form soft peaks. Add the almond extract and orange zest and briefly whisk until the mixture forms stiff peaks when you lift the whisk.

Add the ground almond mixture to the bowl and fold into the meringue, using a large metal spoon or rubber spatula, to make a heavy dough. Cover the bowl and chill for at least 4 hours, or overnight.

When ready to bake, line two baking sheets with baking paper. Lay a large sheet of baking paper on the worktop and dust it with plenty of icing sugar. Put the dough on the paper and shape it into a thin log, rolling it back and forth in the sugar and smoothing out any cracks, until it is about 1.5cm thick and 25cm long. Cut into 25 slices. Put the slices cut side down on the lined baking sheets, setting them well apart, then use your fingers to gently pinch and shape them into neat ovals. Dust with icing sugar, then leave uncovered to dry slightly while you preheat the oven to 180°C: this encourages the tops to crack in the oven.

Bake for about 17–20 minutes until golden and just firm. Leave until cold and firm before removing from the baking sheets.

Store in an airtight container and eat within a week.

Toasted Pecan Chocolate Macarons – French Sandwiched Style

Makes about 10 pairs

100g pecans
75g icing sugar
2 medium egg whites, at room temperature
A large pinch of salt
75g caster sugar
25g cocoa powder

For the ganache filling

75g dark chocolate (about 70 per cent cocoa solids) or good-quality white chocolate
75ml whipping cream

Line two baking sheets with baking paper. Preheat the oven to 180°C.

Put the nuts into an ovenproof dish and toast in the oven for about 5–7 minutes until slightly darker. Meanwhile, draw 20 5cm circles, spaced slightly apart, on the underside of the baking paper.

Leave the nuts to cool. Tip the cooled nuts into a food processor, add the icing sugar and whizz to a fine, sandy powder.

Put the egg whites and salt into a spotlessly clean, grease-free mixing bowl and whisk using an electric mixer until the whites form soft peaks. Whisk in the caster sugar a tablespoon at a time and whisk just until the mixture forms stiff peaks.

Sift the cocoa powder into the bowl, then add the nut mixture and carefully fold everything together using a large metal spoon or rubber spatula.

Spoon a scant 2 teaspoons of the mixture into the centre of each circle on the baking paper and spread to make a neat disc. Bang the baking sheet on the worktop to dislodge any air pockets, then leave uncovered for 15 minutes.

Bake for 15–19 minutes until the macarons feel just firm when gently pressed in the centre – they will firm up as they cool and you want the centres to be slightly soft. Carefully slide the baking paper sheets onto a wire rack and leave until cold before peeling off the macarons.

Meanwhile, make the ganache filling: chop the chocolate very finely and put it into a heatproof bowl. Heat the cream until steaming hot but not quite boiling and then pour it over the chocolate. Leave for a minute, then gently stir until melted and smooth. Set aside until firm enough to spread easily. Use the ganache to sandwich the macarons.

Store in an airtight container and eat within 5 days.

Coconut Kisses – New York Custard-style Macaroons

Makes about 20

For the custard

75ml milk (not skimmed/fat-free)
30g caster sugar
1 tbsp cornflour
1 medium egg yolk
½ tsp vanilla extract

For the coconut mixture

3 medium egg whites, at room temperature
A large pinch of salt
100g caster sugar
200g desiccated coconut

To finish

100g dark chocolate (about 70 per cent cocoa solids)
2 tsp sunflower oil

To make the custard: heat the milk in a small pan until steaming, then remove from the heat. Put the sugar and cornflour into a small heatproof bowl, add the yolk and vanilla and beat well with a wooden spoon until the mixture is pale and smooth. Gradually work in the hot milk, then tip the mixture back into the pan. Set over a low–medium heat and stir briskly with a wire whisk or wooden spoon until the mixture boils and thickens. Turn out onto a plate and press a piece of dampened baking paper onto the surface to prevent a skin from forming; leave until cool.

Line two baking sheets with baking paper and preheat the oven to 160°C.

To make the coconut mixture: put the egg whites and salt into a large mixing bowl and whisk with a fork until frothy. Add the caster sugar and beat with a wooden spoon until combined, then stir in the coconut, followed by the cold custard, until thoroughly combined.

Pack some of the mixture into a tablespoon measure, using a teaspoon, then tap it out onto the lined baking sheet to make a small, rough mound. Repeat with the remaining mixture, setting the mounds well apart.

Bake for about 20 minutes until lightly golden with darker edges (the centres will be sticky). Leave on the baking sheets until completely cold.

To finish: finely chop the chocolate and put it into a small, shallow heatproof bowl. Melt gently, either over a pan of steaming water or in the microwave (see page 10). Remove the bowl from the heat and stir in the oil. One at a time, peel the macaroons off the baking paper and dip the base in the melted chocolate so the chocolate extends 2–3mm up the sides. Leave to set, base side down, on a clean sheet of baking paper.

When set, peel the coconut kisses away from the paper. Store in an airtight container and eat within 4 days.

Mocha Kisses

The name of these rich sandwiched biscuits comes from the port of Mocha in Yemen, once renowned for exporting fine Arabian coffee. These days 'mocha' means a food or drink flavoured with a combination of coffee and chocolate.

The coffee-flavoured biscuits are just as delicious unfilled and are excellent for eating along with ice cream.

Makes 10 pairs

2 tsp instant coffee granules or powder	**For the filling**
2 tsp boiling water	2 tsp instant coffee granules or powder
1 medium egg, at room temperature	2 tsp cocoa powder
180g plain flour	75g unsalted butter, very soft
A large pinch of salt	150g icing sugar, plus extra for dusting
90g caster sugar	2 tbsp finely chopped walnuts (optional)
90g unsalted butter, chilled and diced	

Line two baking sheets with baking paper. Preheat the oven to 170°C.

To make the biscuits: put the coffee into a small bowl; if using granules, crush to a powder with the back of a spoon. Add the boiling water and stir until dissolved, then crack the egg into the bowl and mix thoroughly.

If using a food processor, put the flour, salt and sugar into the processor bowl and pulse briefly, just to combine. Add the butter and process until the mixture looks like breadcrumbs, then add the egg mixture and process just until the mixture comes together.

If using a mixing bowl, combine the flour, salt and sugar in the bowl, then add the butter and rub in using the tips of your fingers, or cut in with a metal pastry blender, until the mixture looks like breadcrumbs. Add the egg mixture and stir in with a round-bladed knife to make a firm dough.

Lightly flour your hands, then pull off small pieces of dough and roll between your hands to make 20 balls the size of large cherries. Set them well apart on the lined baking sheets and bake for about 12–15 minutes until a light golden colour. Leave to firm up for 5 minutes, then transfer to a wire rack and leave until cold.

To make the filling: put the coffee into a mixing bowl; if using granules, crush as before. Add the cocoa powder and butter and beat until creamy using a wooden spoon or electric mixer. Sift the icing sugar into the bowl and beat well – start slowly to avoid a mess – to make a smooth icing with flecks of coffee. Stir in the nuts if using.

Sandwich the cold biscuits in pairs with the filling, then dust lightly with icing sugar. Best eaten the same day, though the unfilled biscuits can be stored in an airtight container for up to 3 days.

Snowy Almond Crescents

These rich, fragile cookies are found all across northern Europe, often baked for celebrations such as weddings and religious holidays. Here, almonds are used, but hazelnuts, walnuts and pecans are also favourites with bakers. For a richer flavour, toast the nuts before grinding with the sugar. For neat results, don't skip the chilling stage.

As with other nut-based biscuits in this chapter, the flavour develops and deepens a day or so after baking.

Makes about 16

125g whole blanched almonds
60g icing sugar, plus extra for dusting
115g unsalted butter or plant butter, chilled and diced

¼ tsp almond extract or ½ tsp brandy
100g plain flour
A large pinch of salt

Tip the almonds and icing sugar into the bowl of a food processor and whizz until the mixture becomes a sandy powder. Scrape down the sides, then add the butter, the almond extract or brandy, the flour and the salt. Pulse a few times just to combine the ingredients, then run the machine until a smooth ball of dough is formed.

Turn out the dough onto a sheet of baking paper and flatten to a thick disc, then wrap and chill for about 30 minutes until firm.

When ready to bake, line two baking sheets with baking paper and preheat the oven to 170°C.

Using a tablespoon measure, scoop out a scant tablespoon of the dough and roll it between your hands to make a sausage about 7cm long. Set it on a lined baking sheet and curve it into a crescent shape. Repeat with the remaining dough, spacing the crescents well apart.

Bake for 15–20 minutes until the edges are barely coloured. Leave the crescents to firm up on the sheets for a few minutes, then transfer to a wire rack to cool.

When completely cold, dust with icing sugar. Store in an airtight container and eat within a week.

Chocolate-dipped Crescents

Gently melt 75g dark or white chocolate (see page 10) in a small deep bowl, then dip one end of each cooled crescent in the melted chocolate and leave to set on a sheet of baking paper. Dust the plain end with icing sugar.

Viennese Whirls

Sometimes called Vienna shortcakes, these are very rich and short-textured piped biscuits, usually sandwiched with jam or chocolate spread. Alternatively, try them filled with clotted cream, fresh sliced berries and a berry jam – perfect for a summer tea in the garden.

The dough needs to be firm enough to pipe, and in order to keep a swirled shape it should be thoroughly chilled before baking.

Makes 10 pairs

225g unsalted butter or plant butter, very soft but not runny
60g icing sugar, plus extra for dusting
¼ tsp vanilla extract
25g cornflour
200g plain flour, sifted
A large pinch of salt
About 100g good jam or chocolate spread

Line two or three baking sheets with baking paper. Draw 20 3.5cm circles, spaced well apart, on the underside of the paper.

Beat the butter with a wooden spoon until creamy. Sift the icing sugar into the bowl, add the vanilla and beat thoroughly. Scrape down the sides of the bowl, then sift the cornflour into the bowl and beat in. Using a wooden spoon or rubber spatula, gradually work in the sifted flour and salt to make a smooth, fairly firm dough.

Transfer the dough to a piping bag fitted with a medium star tube. Pipe swirls within the circles drawn on the baking paper – they will spread. Chill for about 30 minutes until hard.

Meanwhile, preheat the oven to 190°C.

Bake, in batches if necessary, for about 12–15 minutes until pale golden with darker edges. Leave on the baking sheets until completely cold as the biscuits are fragile.

Carefully sandwich in pairs with a little jam or chocolate spread and dust the top with icing sugar. They are best eaten the same day.

West Country Easter Biscuits

With ingredients associated with Easter and the end of Lent, the spices and fruit a link to the Holy Land, these pretty biscuits were often tied with ribbon in stacks of three (to symbolise the Trinity) and given after the Easter service in Christian tradition – before the days of chocolate eggs.

Makes about 12

125g unsalted butter, softened
75g caster sugar, plus extra for sprinkling
Finely grated zest of ½ unwaxed lemon
1 medium egg, separated
200g plain flour, plus extra for dusting
¼ tsp salt
¼ tsp baking powder
½ tsp ground mixed spice
½ tsp ground cinnamon
50g sultanas, raisins, dried cranberries or sour cherries

Line two baking sheets with baking paper. Preheat the oven to 200°C.

Beat the butter with the sugar and lemon zest until creamy, using a wooden spoon or electric mixer. When the mixture looks slightly fluffy, beat in the egg yolk.

Sift the flour, salt, baking powder, mixed spice and cinnamon into the bowl and stir in with a wooden spoon or rubber spatula. Add the dried fruit and mix in using your hands, gently kneading to make a firm dough.

Turn out the dough onto a lightly floured worktop and roll out to about 4mm thick. Stamp out rounds using a 6.5cm round fluted cutter, then gather up the trimmings, roll out again and cut more rounds.

Set the rounds slightly apart on the lined baking sheets, then bake for about 9–10 minutes until firm and golden.

Meanwhile, beat the reserved egg white with a fork until frothy. As soon as the biscuits are ready, remove the baking sheets from the oven and quickly and lightly brush the top of each biscuit with egg white, then sprinkle with a little sugar. Return them to the oven and bake for a further 5 minutes or until the tops are golden and crunchy.

Leave to firm up for about 5 minutes, then transfer to a wire rack to cool.

When completely cold, store in an airtight container and eat within a week.

Shrewsbury Biscuits

Also known as Shrewsbury cakes, near the castle in Shrewsbury there is an old wall plaque marking the spot where a baker named Pailin first made the 'unique Shrewsbury cakes to his original recipe in the year 1760'. However, they seem to have been popular before then, although the original flavourings are not known. A family recipe book dating from the seventeenth century, owned by a Colonel Plomer, notes that they should contain caraway seeds, nutmeg, sack (or sherry) and rosewater; Hannah Woolley writing in 1672 favours cinnamon and rosewater; Eliza Smith, in 1728, insists on nutmeg and cinnamon; and other local recipes from the eighteenth and nineteenth centuries include grated lemon zest. But crucially, all the recipes say the biscuits should be rich, buttery and crisp.

To make Shrewsbury biscuits, follow the recipe as for West Country Easter Biscuits, replacing the lemon zest, mixed spice and cinnamon with ¼ teaspoon freshly grated nutmeg, ½ teaspoon caraway seeds and 1 teaspoon rosewater (not essence). Omit the egg white and sugar topping.

Chapter 4
Squares and Bars

Easy Millionaire's Shortbread

A recipe that 'does what it says on the tin': a classic shortbread base, a sticky fudge layer (made with a tin of caramelised condensed milk – no need to boil in the tin) and a nutty dark chocolate topping.

Makes 16 pieces

For the shortbread base

250g plain flour
A large pinch of salt
A large pinch of grated nutmeg
75g caster sugar
175g unsalted butter, chilled and diced

For the fudge layer

75g unsalted butter, diced
75g light muscovado sugar
397g tin Carnation Caramel (caramelised condensed milk with sugar)
¼ tsp sea salt flakes

For the topping

100g dark chocolate (about 70 per cent cocoa solids), chopped
20g unsalted butter, very soft
50g chopped toasted hazelnuts

Grease a 20cm square tin, about 5cm deep, and line with baking paper, extending the paper over the edges of the tin. Preheat the oven to 180°C.

To make the base in a food processor: put the flour, salt, nutmeg, sugar and butter into the processor bowl and whizz until the mixture looks like coarse breadcrumbs.

To make in a mixing bowl: sift the flour, salt and nutmeg into the bowl, then stir in the sugar. Add the butter and toss until coated, then rub in using the tips of your fingers, or cut in with a metal pastry blender, until the mixture looks like coarse crumbs.

Tip the mixture into the prepared tin and spread it evenly, then lightly press it down using the back of a spoon. Bake for 20–25 minutes until a pale gold colour (you won't need the oven again). Leave to cool in the tin.

Once the base is cold, make the fudge layer. Put the butter, sugar and the caramel into a heavy-based saucepan, preferably non-stick, and heat gently, stirring with a wooden spoon until the butter has melted. Bring to the boil and then, stirring constantly, boil for 5 minutes or until the mixture turns a richer, darker caramel and thickens. Remove from the heat, stir in the sea salt flakes, then pour the boiling mixture over the base and leave to set.

To make the topping: put the chocolate into a heatproof bowl and melt gently, either over a pan of steaming water or in the microwave (see page 10). Remove the bowl from the heat, then stir in the butter and the nuts. Spread the mixture evenly over the fudge layer and leave to set at room temperature.

Remove the whole shortbread from the tin, lifting it using the overhanging paper, and put it on a cutting board. Cut into bars or squares using a large sharp knife dipped into hot water and wiped between each cut.

Store in an airtight container and eat within a week.

Sticky Flapjacks (GF)

An old-fashioned chewy treat, made from porridge oats, golden syrup, muscovado sugar and butter (or plant butter), simply mixed in a saucepan. The nuts add crunch (though you can omit them if preferred), while dried apricots bring a sweet-sour taste; you could also add extra raisins or some chocolate chips.

Makes 12

150g unsalted butter or plant butter, diced
120g light muscovado sugar
35g golden syrup
200g porridge oats (gluten free, if needed)
¼ tsp sea salt flakes
80g chopped mixed nuts (such as cashews, almonds, hazelnuts, pecans, pistachios, Brazil nuts), or chopped dried apricots
1 tbsp raisins

Grease a 20cm square tin and line with baking paper. Preheat the oven to 150°C.

Weigh the butter, sugar and syrup into a saucepan large enough to hold all the ingredients. Set over a low heat and stir with a wooden spoon until the butter has melted.

Remove the pan from the heat and stir in the oats, salt, nuts (or apricots) and raisins until thoroughly combined, and the nuts (or apricots) are evenly distributed. Transfer the mixture to the prepared tin and spread it evenly, then gently press it down using the back of a spoon.

Bake for 20–25 minutes or until golden brown. Put the tin on a wire rack and leave to cool for 10 minutes, then run a round-bladed knife around the inside of the tin to loosen the flapjack and score into 12 bars or squares.

Leave until completely cold before cutting and removing from the tin.

Store in an airtight container and eat within a week.

Tiffin (GF)

There's debate about the origin of the word 'tiffin': according to a late-eighteenth-century dictionary it was 'tiffing', slang for a snack, but a century later it had become the word for a light midday meal in India. For chocolate lovers it means a chilled fridge cake made with crumbled biscuits along with nuts or dried fruit, all stuck together with plenty of melted chocolate. The post-war days of bargain-priced broken biscuits (sold loose from large tins at the grocers) mixed with cocoa powder and margarine have long gone – Prince William and Catherine Middleton chose an extraordinarily rich version, coated in chocolate ganache and decorated, as one of their two wedding cakes in 2011.

The recipe is flexible: you can use any plain, crisp biscuits: Wheaten Biscuits (page 20) are ideal, or otherwise digestives, rich tea or petit beurre. For a deep, rich flavour go for dark chocolate with 70 per cent cocoa solids (or even slightly more for real aficionados), but you could also use a mixture of good milk and dark chocolates for a lighter result (check for vegan-friendly brands), and a mix of nuts and dried fruit or chunks of stem or glacé ginger.

Makes 16 pieces

- 100g mixed unsalted nuts (such as almonds, hazelnuts, pistachios, cashews)
- 200g dark chocolate (see above), broken up
- 100g unsalted butter or plant butter, diced
- 40g golden syrup
- 40g chopped glacé or drained stem ginger, or dried fruit (sour cherries, cranberries, raisins)
- 150g plain biscuits or gluten-free alternative
- Cocoa powder for dusting

Brush a 20cm square tin with vegetable oil, then line with baking paper, extending the paper over two opposite sides of the tin. Preheat the oven to 180°C.

Tip the nuts into an ovenproof dish and toast in the oven for 5–7 minutes until lightly golden. (You won't need the oven again.) Leave to cool, then roughly chop or leave the nuts whole for more texture.

Put the broken-up chocolate into a heatproof bowl large enough to hold all the ingredients and add the butter and golden syrup. Set the bowl over a pan of gently simmering water (don't let the base of the bowl touch the water) and leave to melt, stirring frequently with a wooden spoon.

Once the mixture is smooth take the bowl off the pan and stir in the ginger or dried fruit and the nuts. Break up the biscuits into chunks about the size of your thumbnail – there's no need to be precise here – and stir in. When everything is thoroughly combined, transfer the mixture to the prepared tin and spread evenly. Leave the mixture looking a bit lumpy and bumpy rather than trying to smooth it out neatly. Chill for about 2 hours until firm.

Carefully lift the tiffin out of the tin using the overhanging paper and put it on a cutting board. Cut into squares, then dust with cocoa powder.

Store in an airtight container in the fridge for up to a week, but allow to come back up to room temperature before eating.

Rum and Raisin Tiffin

Use 50g large raisins (rather than ginger or other fruit) and soak them overnight in a couple of tablespoons of dark rum or brandy before adding to the mixture. Cut into smaller squares to make a festive gift.

German Almond and Honey Squares

A recipe from Berlin, these crunchy and slightly sticky squares are popular across Germany. The crisp base layer is baked like a rich shortbread; for the topping the ingredients are combined in a frying pan, added to the base and quickly finished in the oven. Look for a well-flavoured honey rather than a bland or mild type.

Makes 24

For the base
170g plain flour
A large pinch of salt
115g unsalted butter, chilled and diced
30g caster sugar
1 medium egg yolk
½ tsp vanilla extract

For the topping
175g flaked almonds
85g unsalted butter
40g caster sugar
40g set honey
¼ tsp sea salt flakes
2 tbsp single or double cream

Grease a Swiss roll tin or shallow baking tin, about 30 x 20cm, and line with baking paper.

To make the base: sift the flour and salt into a mixing bowl. Add the butter and rub into the flour using your fingertips, or cut in with a metal pastry blender, until the mixture looks like fine crumbs. Stir in the sugar, then add the yolk and the vanilla and work all the ingredients together with your hands to make a fairly firm dough. You could also use a food processor: combine the flour, salt and butter and pulse to make fine crumbs, then add the yolk and vanilla and process to make a smooth, firm dough.

Transfer the dough to the prepared tin. Lightly flour your fingers and gently press the dough over the base of the tin to make an even layer. Prick well with a fork, then chill for 15 minutes.

Meanwhile, preheat the oven to 180°C.

Bake the dough for about 10–12 minutes until firm and golden. Remove from the oven and leave in the tin while you make the topping.

To make the topping: put the flaked almonds, butter, sugar, honey and sea salt flakes into a frying pan, preferably non-stick, and set over a low heat. Stir constantly with a wooden spoon until the butter has melted and the mixture is a pale straw colour. Stir in the cream and cook for 10 seconds, then quickly pour the mixture over the cooked base and spread it evenly.

Return the tin to the oven and bake for 10 minutes or until the mixture turns a glossy golden brown. Leave in the tin until cold, then cut into squares.

Store in an airtight container and eat within 5 days.

Granola Bars (GF)

These crunchy bars, made with porridge oats, are a bit more elaborate than flapjacks, and are packed with your favourite nuts and seeds, flavoured with maple syrup and finished with a little melted chocolate. Puffed rice cereal is added for a lighter, crisper and less dense bar.

Makes 12

- 150g porridge oats (gluten free, if needed)
- 2 tbsp light olive oil or vegetable oil
- 150g coarsely chopped nuts (a mix of almonds, pecans, cashews, cashews, pistachios)
- 40g seeds (a mix of pumpkin, sunflower, linseed, chia)
- 20g puffed rice breakfast cereal (gluten free, if needed)
- ½ tsp ground cinnamon
- ¼ tsp sea salt flakes
- 25g soft-dried sour cherries, cranberries, blueberries or raisins, or a mixture
- 150g pure maple syrup
- 35g unsalted butter or plant butter, diced

To finish

- 75g dark chocolate (about 70 per cent cocoa solids, vegan if preferred), chopped
- 2 tbsp light olive oil or vegetable oil

Preheat the oven to 180°C.

Weigh the oats into an ungreased baking tin, about 20cm square. Sprinkle with the oil, then rub the oats between the palms of your hands until the oats are evenly and lightly coated with oil. Shake the tin to level the oats, then toast in the oven for 10 minutes or until very lightly coloured. Remove the tin from the oven, add the chopped nuts, seeds, puffed rice, cinnamon and salt and mix well.

Return the tin to the oven and toast for another 10 minutes or until the cinnamon smells 'toasty' and the mixture looks golden. Remove the tin from the oven, add the dried fruit and stir well. Tip the mixture into a large mixing bowl and leave to cool.

Reduce the oven temperature to 170°C. Wipe out the tin, then lightly grease and line the base with baking paper.

Weigh the maple syrup and butter into a small pan and set over a low heat until melted, then bring to the boil and simmer for 1 minute. Pour the butter mixture over the oat mixture and mix thoroughly. Transfer to the prepared tin and spread evenly, right into the corners, then gently level the surface without compressing the mixture.

Bake for about 18–22 minutes until lightly golden with slightly darker edges. Put the tin on a wire rack and run a round-bladed knife around the inside of the tin to loosen the mixture. Leave until just warm, then cut into bars using a large sharp knife. Leave in the tin until cold.

To finish: put the chocolate into a heatproof bowl and melt gently, either over a pan of steaming water or in the microwave (see page 10). Remove the bowl from the heat, stir gently, then stir in the oil and leave to cool until thick enough to pipe. Spoon into a small piping bag, or a small plastic bag and snip off the tip, then pipe over the bars in a zigzag pattern. Alternatively, you can drip or drizzle the chocolate onto the bars from a spoon. Leave to set, then slice along the cut lines again with a sharp knife and remove from the tin.

Store in an airtight container and eat within a week.

Grasmere Ginger Shortbread

If you are visiting Allan Bank in the Lake District, once home to William Wordsworth, you will be near the village of Grasmere. The village has been famous for its versions of gingerbread or ginger shortbread since the mid-eighteenth century; Dorothy Wordsworth wrote about the thick and thin types of gingerbread she was offered while living at Dove Cottage. Recipes for these shortbreads appear to have developed with the arrival of Jamaican sugar and spices that came through the nearby port of Whitehaven as part of the transatlantic slave trade.

The most famous version is Sarah Nelson's Grasmere Gingerbread (a trademark). Born in 1815 in Bowness-on-Windermere, Sarah Nelson worked her way up from domestic servant to cook for Lady Maria Farquhar in Grasmere. By 1854 she had developed a spicy, chewy, crunchy recipe that was a cross between a flapjack and sandy shortbread, and began selling her now-famous Grasmere Gingerbread to locals and tourists. Still baked and sold in Grasmere, the recipe is a trade secret, kept in a bank vault and still intriguing bakers and customers over 120 years after her death.

Makes 16 squares

200g plain flour
50g fine oatmeal
125g light muscovado sugar
¼ tsp salt
1½ tsp ground ginger
½ tsp bicarbonate of soda

150g unsalted butter or plant butter, chilled and diced
25g (1 large lump) stem ginger, well drained, or glacé ginger, finely chopped

Grease a 20cm square tin and line with baking paper, extending the paper over two opposite sides of the tin. Preheat the oven to 180°C.

To make in a food processor: tip the flour, oatmeal, sugar, salt, ground ginger and bicarbonate of soda into the processor bowl and pulse until combined. Add the butter and process just until the mixture looks sandy – don't overwork the ingredients or they clump together.

To make in a mixing bowl: combine all the dry ingredients and mix well. Add the butter and toss until coated, then rub in between the tips of your fingers, or cut in with a metal pastry blender, until the mixture looks like sandy crumbs.

Remove 4 tablespoons of the sandy crumbs and set aside for the topping.

Add the finely chopped ginger to the remaining mixture in the processor or mixing bowl and briefly pulse, or mix until thoroughly combined.

Tip the mixture into the prepared tin and spread it evenly, then press it down firmly using the back of a spoon. Scatter the reserved crumbs on top. Using a round-bladed knife, gently score the shortbread into 16 squares.

Bake for about 25 minutes until lightly golden. Remove from the oven and – leaving the shortbread in the tin – carefully cut along the scored lines. Put the tin on a wire rack and leave until cold before lifting out the squares, using the overhanging paper to help.

Store in an airtight container and eat within a week.

Lemon Squares

According to food historians, a lemon-topped shortcake was a favourite of the royal court at Kew Palace in the late eighteenth century.

In this recipe a crisp shortbread base is baked a second time with a sticky, sharp-sweet lemon topping. Both elements are easy to make in a food processor or in a mixing bowl. Adding pistachio nuts makes a more glamorous version (see below).

Makes 16 squares

For the base

125g plain flour
A large pinch of salt
35g icing sugar
100g unsalted butter, chilled and diced

For the topping

2 medium eggs, at room temperature
125g caster sugar
15g plain flour
½ tsp baking powder
A large pinch of sea salt flakes, or to taste
Finely grated zest and juice of 2 unwaxed lemons
Icing sugar for dusting

Grease a 20cm square tin and line with baking paper, extending the paper over two opposite sides of the tin. Preheat the oven to 180°C.

To make the base in a food processor: put the flour, salt and sugar into the processor bowl and pulse to combine. Add the butter and process just until the mixture looks like fine, sandy crumbs. To make in a mixing bowl: sift the flour, salt and sugar into the bowl, then rub in the butter between the tips of your fingers, or cut in with a metal pastry blender.

Tip the sandy mixture into the prepared tin and spread evenly, then press it down firmly using the back of a spoon.

Bake for 13–16 minutes until firm and a light golden colour with slightly darker edges. Leave to cool while you make the topping.

To make the topping in a processor: put all the ingredients into the processor bowl and process for about 10 seconds until thoroughly combined. Alternatively, put all the ingredients into a mixing bowl and mix thoroughly using a hand whisk.

Pour the slightly foamy mixture over the base, return the tin to the oven and bake for 15–18 minutes until set and pale gold. Leave until completely cold before carefully removing from the tin and cutting into squares, using the overhanging paper to help. Dust with icing sugar.

Store in an airtight container and eat within 4 days.

Lemon Pistachio Squares

You will need 100g pistachio kernels – if you have the time and patience, it is worth blanching them to emphasise their bright green colour. To do this, put them into a small pan, cover with cold water and bring slowly to the boil. Drain, then tip onto a clean dry tea towel and rub quite vigorously to dislodge the papery brown skins. Leave on a dry towel or kitchen paper until completely dry.

Finely chop 20g of the pistachios and mix into the sandy mixture for the base before it goes into the tin, then press down and bake as above. Roughly chop the remaining nuts and mix into the lemon topping mixture with an extra pinch of sea salt flakes, then pour over the base and bake as above.

Raspberry Crumbles

An easy recipe perfect for jam tart fans: a buttery biscuit base with a layer of raspberry conserve or jam, and a crunchy, nutty crumble topping. For a change, black cherry conserve is also delicious here.

Makes 24 bars

For the base

125g plain flour
A large pinch of salt
45g caster sugar
90g unsalted butter or plant butter, chilled and diced

For the topping

85g plain flour
¼ tsp sea salt flakes
30g porridge oats
45g dark muscovado sugar
A little grated nutmeg
60g unsalted butter or plant butter
50g blanched hazelnuts or almonds, roughly chopped
200g good raspberry conserve or jam
Icing sugar for dusting

Grease a 20cm square tin and line with baking paper, extending the paper over two opposite sides of the tin. Preheat the oven to 180°C.

To make the base in a food processor: put the flour, salt and sugar into the processor bowl and pulse a few times to combine, then add the butter and pulse until the mixture looks like breadcrumbs.

To make the base in a mixing bowl: sift the flour, salt and sugar into the bowl, then rub in the butter between the tips of your fingers, or cut in with a metal pastry blender, until the mixture looks like crumbs.

Tip the mixture into the prepared tin and spread it evenly, then press it down firmly using the back of a spoon.

Bake for about 20 minutes until lightly coloured. Leave to cool while you make the topping.

Put the flour, salt, oats, sugar and nutmeg into a mixing bowl and mix everything together with your fingers, pressing out any small lumps of sugar. Melt the butter and drizzle it over the ingredients, then use your fingers to work it in to make pea-sized pieces of dough. Stir in the chopped nuts.

Spread the jam over the base, in an even layer, then scatter evenly with the crumble topping.

Bake for about 35 minutes until the topping is lightly browned and the jam is starting to bubble through. Put the tin on a wire rack and leave until cold before removing from the tin, using the overhanging paper to help. Cut into bars and dust with icing sugar.

Store in an airtight container and eat within 5 days.

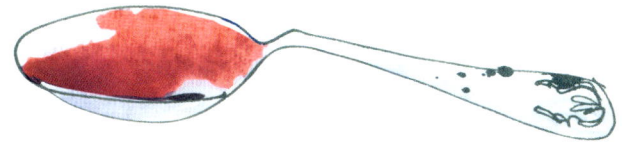

Chapter 5
Biscotti

Cinnamon and Raisin Biscotti

This is a classic flavour combination for *biscotti*, the Italian twice-baked biscuit – the name is derived from the Latin *panis biscotus* or twice-cooked bread. These have a sweet, crisp crumb and a nutty crunch; they are made in the traditional way using an egg but no butter – perfect for dipping in coffee, hot chocolate or *vin santo* dessert wine.

For the initial bake the dough is shaped into a flattish loaf; once cooked it is cut into diagonal slices which are then baked a second time at a lower temperature to dry and crisp the biscuits.

Makes about 20

50g whole blanched almonds
1 medium egg, at room temperature
100g caster sugar
½ tsp vanilla extract
130g plain flour, plus extra for dusting

A large pinch of salt
½ tsp baking powder
½ tsp ground cinnamon
50g raisins

Line a baking sheet with baking paper. Preheat the oven to 180°C.

Toast the almonds in an ovenproof dish for 10–15 minutes until lightly coloured. Set aside and leave to cool.

Break the egg into a large mixing bowl, then add the sugar and vanilla. Whisk with an electric mixer for 3–4 minutes until the mixture is thick and mousse-like.

Sift the flour, salt, baking powder and cinnamon onto a sheet of baking paper, then sift again into the mixing bowl and stir in until thoroughly combined. Add the raisins and toasted nuts and mix until evenly distributed.

Scoop out the dough onto the lined baking sheet, lightly flour your hands, then shape the dough into a flattish loaf about 24 x 7.5cm and 2cm thick. Bake for 20–25 minutes until a light golden colour and just firm to the touch.

Leave to cool for 10 minutes, then transfer to a cutting board and reduce the oven temperature to 150°C. Line the baking sheet with a fresh sheet of baking paper.

Using a serrated bread knife and a gentle sawing motion, cut the baked dough on a slight diagonal into 1cm thick slices. Lay the slices on the baking sheet and bake for 10–15 minutes until lightly coloured and just firm and crisp. Leave on the baking sheet for 5 minutes, then transfer to a wire rack to cool.

When completely cold, store in an airtight container or glass storage jar. Best eaten within a week.

Pistachio Biscotti

Vivid green pistachios look impressive in pale biscotti slices. They find a perfect partner here in dark, soft-dried sour cherries, whose unique flavour is a fine, unexpected combination of tartness and sweetness.

Makes about 30

50g unsalted butter
225g plain flour, plus extra for dusting
½ tsp baking powder
A large pinch of salt
150g caster sugar

2 medium eggs
¼ tsp almond extract
60g soft-dried sour cherries
100g pistachio kernels, roughly chopped

Line two baking sheets with baking paper. Preheat the oven to 180°C.

Melt the butter over a low heat, then set aside.

Sift the flour, baking powder, salt and sugar into a large mixing bowl, then make a well in the centre. Beat the eggs with the almond extract in a small bowl, then pour into the well, followed by the melted butter. Mix well, then add the cherries and pistachios and work in until evenly distributed.

Turn out the dough onto a lightly floured worktop and gently knead for a few seconds, then divide the dough in half and put each piece of dough onto a lined baking sheet. Lightly flour your hands, then shape each piece of dough into a flattish loaf about 20 x 7.5cm and 2cm thick. Bake for 20–25 minutes until a light golden colour and just firm to the touch.

Leave to cool for 10 minutes, then transfer one loaf to a cutting board and reduce the oven temperature to 150°C. Line the baking sheet with a fresh sheet of baking paper.

Using a serrated bread knife, cut the baked dough on a slight diagonal into 1cm thick slices. Lay the slices on the baking sheet. Repeat with the second baked loaf, then bake for 15–20 minutes until the slices are lightly coloured, firm and dry. Leave on the baking sheets for 5 minutes, then transfer to a wire rack to cool.

When completely cold, store in an airtight container or glass storage jar. Best eaten within a week.

Toasted Almond and Fig Biscotti

The beauty of biscotti is not only that they are easy to make but also that they lend themselves to adaptation and experimentation. This traditional fruit and nut combo can be left plain and simple or you can include your own flavourings: add ¼ teaspoon almond or vanilla extract along with the eggs; or add ½ teaspoon ground cinnamon or ¼ teaspoon ground cardamom seeds with the flour; or perhaps ¼ teaspoon finely chopped fresh rosemary or culinary lavender with the fruit and chopped nuts.

Makes about 26

85g whole blanched almonds
120g soft-dried figs
120g unsalted butter, softened
125g caster sugar
2 medium eggs, beaten

300g plain flour, plus extra for dusting
A large pinch of salt
½ tsp baking powder

Line two baking sheets with baking paper. Preheat the oven to 180°C.

Toast the almonds in an ovenproof dish for 10–15 minutes until lightly coloured. Leave to cool, then roughly chop. Chop the figs into chunks of about the same size, then set both aside.

In a large mixing bowl, beat the butter with a wooden spoon or electric mixer until creamy. Scrape down the sides of the bowl, add the sugar and beat until light and fluffy. Gradually beat in the eggs, then sift the flour, salt and baking powder into the bowl. Mix everything together with a wooden spoon to make a slightly sticky dough, then work in the chopped figs and nuts until thoroughly combined.

Divide the dough in half and put each piece onto a lined baking sheet. Lightly flour your hands, then shape each piece of dough into a flattish loaf about 24 x 7.5cm and 2cm thick. Bake for about 25 minutes or until a light golden colour and just firm.

Leave to cool for 10 minutes, then transfer one loaf to a cutting board and reduce the oven temperature to 150°C. Line the baking sheet with a fresh sheet of baking paper.

Using a serrated bread knife, cut the baked dough on a slight diagonal into 1cm thick slices. Lay the slices on the baking sheet. Repeat with the second baked loaf, then bake for about 10–15 minutes until the slices are lightly coloured, firm and crisp. Leave on the baking sheets for 5 minutes, then transfer to a wire rack to cool.

When completely cold, store in an airtight container and eat within a week.

Triple Chocolate Biscotti

These are the ultimate in richly flavoured biscotti: made without nuts but with cocoa powder and chocolate pieces added to the dough, and finished with a dip into melted dark chocolate.

Makes about 36

125g dark chocolate (around 70 per cent cocoa solids) or milk chocolate (around 40 per cent cocoa solids), in a bar, drops or chips
100g unsalted butter
3 medium eggs, at room temperature
200g light muscovado sugar
Finely grated zest of ½ unwaxed orange

325g plain flour, plus extra for dusting
2 tsp baking powder
25g cocoa powder
¼ tsp sea salt flakes

To finish

150g dark or good white chocolate (at least 30 per cent cocoa butter)

Line two baking sheets with baking paper. Preheat the oven to 180°C.

If you are using a bar of chocolate, rather than drops or chips, chop it into chunks about the size of your little fingernail and set aside.

Melt the butter over a low heat, then set aside until just lukewarm.

Meanwhile, break the eggs into a large mixing bowl and whisk with an electric mixer for a couple of minutes until frothy. Add the sugar and orange zest; whisk for 3–4 minutes until the mixture is thick and foamy, then gradually whisk in the melted butter. Whisk for another minute, then scrape down the sides of the bowl.

Sift the flour, baking powder and cocoa powder into the bowl and mix in with a wooden spoon or rubber spatula. As soon as the mixture is evenly combined with no floury streaks, add the salt and chocolate and work in to make a heavy, rather sticky dough.

Divide the dough in half and put each piece onto a lined baking sheet. Lightly flour your hands, then shape each piece of dough into a flattish loaf about 24 x 7.5cm x 2cm thick.

Bake for 25 minutes or until just firm when gently pressed in the centre – the dough will continue cooking for a few minutes after it comes out of the oven. Leave until completely cold (you can turn off the oven for now) – don't attempt to slice the baked dough at this point, as the chocolate will be molten.

When you are ready for the second bake, heat the oven to 150°C. Transfer one loaf to a cutting board and line the baking sheet with a fresh sheet of baking paper. Using a serrated bread knife and a gentle sawing motion, cut the baked dough on a slight diagonal into 1cm thick slices. Lay the slices on the baking sheet. Repeat with the second baked loaf, then bake for about 18–20 minutes until firm and dry. Leave on the baking sheets for 5 minutes, then transfer to a wire rack until completely cold. Keep the lined baking sheets for finishing the biscotti.

To finish: chop or break the chocolate into even-sized pieces and put into a small, deep heatproof bowl. Melt gently, either over a pan of steaming water or in the microwave (see page 10). Remove the bowl from the heat and give the chocolate a gentle stir. Dip one end of each biscotti (about a third) into the chocolate so it is very lightly coated – let the excess drip back into the bowl, then leave to set on the lined baking sheets.

Store in an airtight container and eat within a week.

Sea Salt Praline Biscotti

Praline was invented, it is said by accident, in the Loire region of France, early in the seventeenth century. The legend is that children playing in the servants' quarters of the Duke of Choiseul-Praslin at Montargis accidentally burnt some sugared almonds; the delicious results were perfected in the pastry kitchens and then taken to the court of Louis XIII. The confectioner responsible eventually retired back to Montargis and opened a shop, which you can visit today – they claim their recipe is practically unchanged since 1636.

In this recipe, the praline is made with hazelnuts cooked with sugar to a bitter-sweet caramel, which sets hard and is then broken up and added to the biscotti dough.

Makes about 34

For the praline
100g caster sugar
100g blanched hazelnuts
¼ tsp sea salt flakes

For the biscotti dough
150g unsalted butter, softened
200g caster sugar
1 medium egg, plus 1 yolk
375g plain flour, plus extra for dusting
2 tsp baking powder

First, make the praline: oil a baking sheet, then put the sugar and nuts into a heavy-based saucepan; have the oiled baking sheet nearby. Set the pan over a very low heat and leave the sugar to melt, swirling and shaking the pan to help it melt evenly – you can stir very gently with a metal spoon to move the mixture from the sides to the middle of the pan. Once the sugar has completely melted, turn up the heat so the syrup bubbles and starts to darken – again, stir gently now and then so the nuts brown on all sides.

Once the caramel turns chestnut brown (and smells of caramel), quickly tip the mixture onto the oiled baking sheet and spread with a metal spoon, then scatter with the sea salt flakes. Leave until completely cold.

Break up the praline into chunks, then pulse in a food processor to make large crumbs with a few bigger lumps. Alternatively, transfer the praline to a sturdy, reusable plastic bag, close tightly and then bash with a rolling pin. Set aside.

Preheat the oven to 180°C. Line two baking sheets with baking paper.

To make the biscotti: beat the butter in a mixing bowl with a wooden spoon or electric whisk until creamy, then gradually beat in the sugar until thoroughly combined. In a small bowl, beat the egg and yolk together, then beat into the creamed mixture.

Sift the flour and baking powder into the bowl and mix in with a rubber spatula or a wooden spoon. Add the praline and work in until evenly distributed, then use your hands to bring the dough together. Divide the dough in half and put each piece on a lined baking sheet. Lightly flour your hands, then shape each piece of dough into a flattish loaf about 30 x 7.5cm and 2cm thick.

Bake for about 30 minutes until golden and just firm – the dough will spread slightly as it bakes. Leave on the baking sheets to firm up for 10 minutes. Reduce the oven temperature to 150°C.

Slide the biscotti, still on the baking paper, onto a cutting board and line the baking sheets with fresh baking paper. Using a serrated bread knife, cut on a slight diagonal into slices about

1cm thick. Lay the slices on the baking sheet. Repeat with the second biscotti, then bake for about 20 minutes until crisp and a light golden colour. Transfer to a wire rack to cool.

When completely cold, store in an airtight container or glass storage jar. Best eaten within a week.

Chapter 6
Savoury

Cheese Marmite Walnut Coins

The recipe for these very moreish biscuits comes from the food writer Jenny Linford, author of *The Great British Food Tour* (which includes an entry on the history of Marmite). They are perfect with drinks and nibbles, and can be made well in advance.

The method is easy; the mixture needs to be chilled before slicing and baking but will keep in the freezer for a couple of weeks.

A yeast extract spread (what we know today as Marmite) made from a concentrated form of brewer's yeast was invented towards the end of the nineteenth century by a German scientist. In 1902 the first factory to produce Marmite was constructed in Burton upon Trent, in Staffordshire, using the lees (a by-product of beer-brewing) from the local Bass Brewery. As well as its distinctive savoury taste, Marmite is now known as a source of vitamins: its vitamin B is supposed to have helped troops overcome beriberi during the First World War.

Makes about 40

- 50g unsalted butter, at room temperature
- 1 tsp Marmite
- 75g plain flour
- 1 tsp baking powder
- 50g mature Cheddar, finely grated
- 50g Parmesan or Grana Padano, finely grated
- 30g walnut pieces, finely chopped or lightly crushed
- 1–2 tbsp sesame seeds, for coating

Weigh the butter onto a small plate, add the Marmite and mash them together until well combined. Put the plate into the fridge and leave for about 15 minutes until firm.

Sift the flour and baking powder into a mixing bowl. Cut the butter into small flakes, add to the bowl and toss in the flour until coated. Using the tips of your fingers, rub the butter into the flour, or cut in with a metal pastry blender, until the mixture looks like coarse crumbs.

Stir in both cheeses and the nuts, then sprinkle 1 tablespoon cold water over the mixture and work everything together using a round-bladed knife. When the mixture starts to form clumps, use your hands to lightly knead it to make a dough.

Divide the dough in half. Lightly sprinkle a sheet of baking paper with sesame seeds and shape one portion of the dough on the paper to form a log about 2.5cm across and 10cm long, coated with seeds. Repeat with the second portion of dough, then wrap both in the paper and chill for 30 minutes. At this point the dough can be frozen, tightly wrapped (see page 11) for 2 weeks; thaw overnight in the fridge.

When ready to bake, line two baking sheets with baking paper and preheat the oven to 200°C.

Cut the logs into 5mm thick slices and lay the slices slightly apart on the baking sheets. Bake for 10–15 minutes until a rich golden brown. Leave to firm up for 5 minutes, then transfer to a wire rack and leave until cold.

Store in an airtight container and eat within a week.

Cheese Shortbread

This classic, rich cheese biscuit recipe uses equal parts of flour, fat and strongly flavoured hard cheese; add a dash of cayenne pepper or hot smoked paprika to taste. It's quickly made in a food processor.

100g plain flour
100g unsalted butter, chilled and diced
100g Parmesan or Grana Padano, finely grated

Put all the ingredients into a processor and whizz until the mixture comes together. Alternatively, in a mixing bowl, rub the butter into the flour, then add the cheese and knead everything together. Finish the recipe as instructed for the Cheese Marmite Walnut Coins on the previous page, resuming from dividing the dough in half, with or without the sesame seeds.

Oatcakes (GF)

For centuries, oatmeal was a staple in the Pennines, Lake District, Scottish Highlands and North West of England, where it was too damp and chilly for wheat to thrive, and wheat flour was an expensive treat. For centuries, a sack of oatmeal formed a part of the wages for those working the land – farmworkers, crofters and keepers – in Scotland. Oatmeal was made into porridge, puddings and haggis, fried up with onions for skirlie, and added to thicken stews and soups. Oatcakes were eaten with broths, and could be wrapped to take out on the hills.

The recipe is straightforward, but as the main ingredient is oatmeal, which is naturally gluten free (see page 9), the mixture can be prone to crumble when rolled out so needs careful handling. A little fat is added for flavouring – traditionally bacon fat or dripping, but now often butter or plant butter – and the boiling water used for mixing the dough is released as steam during baking, giving a lighter, less dense texture.

The old recipe is certainly well worth making: oatcakes are still very popular, as much with dips and cheeses as with jam or honey for tea.

Makes about 12

- 225g medium oatmeal (gluten free, if needed)
- 2 tbsp oat flour or plain flour, plus extra for dusting
- ¼ tsp light muscovado sugar
- ½ tsp sea salt flakes
- A large pinch of baking powder
- 30g bacon fat, dripping, unsalted butter or plant butter, melted
- 85–125ml boiling water

Lightly grease a baking sheet or line it with baking paper. Preheat the oven to 180°C.

Transfer the oatmeal into an ovenproof dish and toast in the oven for about 10 minutes until very lightly coloured.

Tip the oatmeal into a mixing bowl, add the flour, sugar, salt and baking powder and mix well. Make a well in the centre and pour in the melted fat, followed by 85ml boiling water. Using a round-bladed knife, work in the dry ingredients, adding enough extra boiling water to bind the mixture together – it will firm up as you work, but you are after a dough that is neither sticky nor dry and crumbly. Gently knead the dough in the bowl for a minute, adding more water a teaspoon at a time if it starts to fall apart.

Lightly dust the worktop with flour and roll out the dough to 5mm thick. Stamp out rounds using a 7–7.5cm plain round cutter and transfer them to the prepared baking sheet. Gather up the trimmings, knead them together (adding a little more water if needed), then roll out again and cut more rounds.

Bake the oatcakes for about 20 minutes until firm and crisp. Leave until cold before removing from the baking sheet.

Store in an airtight container. Best eaten within a couple of weeks.

Olive Oil Thins with Rosemary, Za'atar or Dukkah

Paper-thin and very crisp, these oval crackers are ideal for dips and with Middle Eastern dishes. You can flavour the dough with rosemary or sprinkle after shaping with your own favourite toppings – chopped fresh rosemary, a spicy, crunchy mix of herbs and spices such as za'atar, or a warm, nutty one like dukkah are good, as are sesame seeds.

Makes 20

200g plain flour, plus extra for dusting
¾ tsp baking powder
½ tsp icing sugar
½ tsp sea salt flakes, or to taste
1 tsp finely chopped fresh rosemary (optional)

1½ tbsp olive oil
About 100ml water, at room temperature
About 1 tbsp chopped fresh rosemary, za'atar, dukkah or sesame seeds for sprinkling

---

Sift the flour, baking powder and sugar into a mixing bowl. Add the salt and rosemary, if using, and mix in. Make a well in the centre and pour in the oil. Using a round-bladed knife or your hand, start to mix the dough, gradually adding enough water to make a soft but not sticky dough.

Lightly dust the worktop and your hands with flour, then turn out the dough. Knead it for a few seconds, then shape it into a sausage, 20cm long. Wrap and chill for 1 hour.

When ready to bake, line two baking sheets with baking paper and preheat the oven to 220°C.

Put the dough on a cutting board and cut into 20 equal pieces. Lightly dust the worktop and your rolling pin with flour, then roll out each piece of dough to a long, very thin oval – aim for about 15cm long, with a rustic rather than neat shape. Arrange the ovals slightly apart on the lined baking sheets. Sprinkle with your chosen topping and gently press it into the dough.

Bake for 8–10 minutes until lightly coloured with a few bubbles – check after 6 minutes and rotate the sheets if necessary so the crackers colour evenly. Leave to firm up for a couple of minutes, then transfer to a wire rack to cool.

When completely cold, store in an airtight container and eat within 5 days.

Parmesan Palmiers (GF)

Palmiers are traditionally sugary, crisp puff pastries, said to resemble a palm leaf. In this recipe they are made with cheese and mustard – best eaten warm with drinks, soups and salads.

Makes about 32

320g ready-rolled puff pastry sheet (all butter, dairy free or gluten free)
100g Parmesan or Grana Padano, finely grated, or vegan alternative
½ tsp sweet or mild paprika
¼ tsp cayenne pepper or ground black pepper, or to taste
1 tbsp Dijon mustard

Follow the pack instructions to ensure the pastry is at the correct temperature (thaw if frozen). When ready to use, unroll the sheet, leaving it on its lining paper. Combine the grated cheese, paprika and cayenne pepper.

Using a round-bladed knife, spread the mustard evenly over the pastry, then scatter the cheese mixture over the top. Mark the centre point on each of the two short sides.

Now roll up the pastry: starting with one long side, gently roll it up towards the centre of the sheet, not too tightly as you want the pastry layers to expand and puff in the oven. Repeat with the other side so the rolls almost meet in the centre. Gently fold one roll on top of the other to make a log shape about 23 x 35cm. Wrap in the lining paper and chill for 30 minutes.

Line two baking sheets with baking paper. Unwrap the log from the paper and put it on a cutting board. Using a large sharp knife, trim the ends and then cut the log into slices about 1cm thick.

Set well apart on the lined baking sheets, then chill for 15 minutes. Meanwhile, preheat the oven to 220°C.

Bake the palmiers for about 9–12 minutes until golden brown and puffed. Remove the baking sheets from the oven and use a palette knife to flip the palmiers over, then bake for a further 3 minutes or so, until both sides are crisp and a rich golden brown. Leave to firm up for a couple of minutes, then serve warm or transfer to a wire rack to cool.

Once cold, store in an airtight container and eat within a couple of days – gently warm before serving.

Black Olive Palmiers

Instead of mustard and cheese, the pastry is spread with tapenade, a richly flavoured spread from Provence made from chopped black olives, garlic, olive oil and capers – some recipes include anchovies, so check the ingredients listed on the jar if you want a vegetarian or vegan version.

Make the palmiers as instructed for Parmesan Palmiers, but replace all the filling ingredients with 140g jar tapenade (about 8 tablespoons), stirring the mixture well before spreading it onto the pastry in an even layer.

Sweet Palmiers

Replace the savoury filling with 3 tablespoons caster sugar mixed with 1 teaspoon ground cinnamon – these palmiers will colour more quickly in the oven.

Polenta Cracked Black Pepper Crackers

This dough is made with a mix of polenta and plain flour and flavoured with olive oil, plus black pepper for a robust warmth. A touch of dried yeast adds lightness, helping the crackers puff up a little during baking. They are good with cheeses, dips, terrines and pâtés.

Makes 48

½ tsp black peppercorns, or to taste
25g polenta
200g plain flour, plus extra for dusting
½ tsp salt
¼ tsp fast-action dried yeast (from a 7g sachet)

3 tbsp olive oil
About 100ml lukewarm water
Sea salt flakes or sesame seeds for sprinkling

Smash the peppercorns fairly coarsely, using a pestle and mortar, or the end of a rolling pin in a sturdy container, or a spice grinder. Put into a mixing bowl with the polenta, flour and salt and mix well. Mix in the dried yeast.

Make a well in the centre of the mixture, pour in the oil and 100ml lukewarm water and work everything together using a round-bladed knife, adding more water as needed to make a fairly firm dough. Knead the dough in the bowl using your hands just for a minute or until it feels smooth and pliable. Cover the bowl and leave at room temperature for an hour to allow the dough to relax (it won't expand).

Line two baking sheets with baking paper and preheat the oven to 190°C.

Lightly dust the worktop and your rolling pin with flour, then roll out the dough to a thin square about 36 x 36cm. Cover the dough with a clean, dry tea towel and leave it to relax for 10 minutes.

Using a pizza wheel cutter, or a large sharp knife and a ruler, trim the sides to neaten, then prick the dough all over with a fork. Brush very lightly with water, then sprinkle with salt flakes or sesame seeds. Cut into 5cm squares and transfer to the lined baking sheets – the crackers will puff slightly but will not spread in the oven.

Bake for about 12–15 minutes until a good golden brown – check after 10 minutes and rotate the sheets if necessary so the crackers colour evenly. Transfer to a wire rack to cool.

When completely cold, store in an airtight container and eat within a week.

Sage and Pecan Biscuits

A combination of British blue cheese, pecans and fresh sage make these rectangular biscuits look and taste very appealing. They are a perfect accompaniment to party drinks, and to soups and salads, but probably a little over the top for a cheeseboard.

Choose your favourite piquant blue cheese, one that's crumbly and well-flavoured – the last of the Christmas Stilton perhaps, or the colourful, creamy, vegetarian Blacksticks Blue from Lancashire. The dough is made in a food processor and needs time in the fridge before baking; it can be stored in the freezer, tightly wrapped, for a week.

Makes about 50

300g plain flour, plus extra for dusting
½ tsp sea salt flakes
¼ tsp ground black pepper
100g pecan halves
5 fresh sage leaves
150g unsalted butter, chilled and diced
50g blue cheese
2 medium eggs, beaten

Put the flour, salt and pepper into the food processor and pulse just to combine. Add the pecans and sage leaves and pulse until roughly chopped, then add the butter and pulse until the mixture looks like coarse crumbs. Crumble the cheese (pea-sized lumps work best) into the mixture, add the eggs, then pulse several times until the mixture comes together.

Turn out the dough and put it on a sheet of baking paper. Flour your hands and shape the dough into a brick about 28 x 7.5 x 2.5cm. Wrap tightly and chill for a couple of hours – the dough, well wrapped (see page 11), can be kept in the fridge for a day, or a week in the freezer (thaw overnight in the fridge).

When ready to bake, line two baking sheets with baking paper and preheat the oven to 180°C.

Cut the dough into slices about 5mm thick and set slightly apart on the lined baking sheets. Bake for 16–20 minutes until golden with slightly darker edges. Leave to firm up for a couple of minutes, then transfer to a wire rack to cool.

When completely cold, store in an airtight container and eat within a week.

Cheese Biscotti

These spicy cheesy biscuits are twice-baked in the same way as their sweet cousins; they are good with drinks or as a base for canapés. Top with diced tomatoes and tiny 'pearl' mozzarella, or slices of pear and blue cheese, or serve with cold soups and salads.

Makes about 18

50g walnut pieces
100g extra mature Cheddar, finely grated
25g Parmesan or Grana Padano, finely grated
150g plain flour, plus extra for dusting
½ tsp caster sugar
½ tsp baking powder
¼ tsp salt
½ tsp smoked mild paprika
¼ tsp cayenne pepper, or to taste
2 medium eggs, beaten

Line a baking sheet with baking paper. Preheat the oven to 180°C.

Put the walnuts into a mixing bowl and gently crush with the end of a rolling pin to break them up slightly without reducing them to powder.

Add both cheeses to the bowl, then add the flour, sugar, baking powder, salt, paprika and cayenne. Mix everything together until thoroughly combined, then make a well in the centre.

Pour the eggs into the well, then mix in using a round-bladed knife to make a dough that's slightly soft but not sticky.

Lightly flour your hands and gently knead the dough in the bowl for a couple of minutes until firm but not dry, adding more flour if you need to stop the dough sticking. Flour your hands again, transfer the dough to the lined baking sheet and gently shape it to a flattish loaf about 24 x 7.5cm and 2cm thick.

Bake for 25–30 minutes until golden brown. Remove from the oven – leave the oven on – and leave to cool for 10 minutes.

Transfer the baked dough to a cutting board. Using a serrated bread knife and a gentle sawing motion, cut on a slight diagonal into 1cm thick slices. Lay the slices on the baking sheet and return to the oven for about 10 minutes until starting to colour. Remove the sheet from the oven and use a palette knife to turn the slices over, then bake for a further 5–6 minutes or until the slices are firm and golden. Transfer to a wire rack to cool.

When completely cold, store in an airtight container and eat within 5 days.

Wholemeal Cream Crackers

In Britain, cracker biscuits often mean just one thing – Jacob's Cream Crackers. The recipe was invented in Dublin in 1885 by William Jacob, who wanted a biscuit that would stay crisp (sounding a 'crack' when snapped) and that he could sell locally and also on the rapidly growing export market. He toured various manufacturers in America, and then devised his own cracker, made from flour and salt with a little fat and milk, rolled very thinly, cut into squares, 'docked' (pricked all over), then baked until crisp and golden. He even designed a box for them that could be tightly sealed to survive long sea voyages.

This is a simple recipe for cheeseboard crackers, using wholemeal flour for a warm, nutty flavour.

Makes 24–30

125g fine plain wholemeal flour (not strong bread flour), plus extra for dusting
½ tsp caster sugar
15g unsalted butter, firm but not fridge-cold
½ tsp sea salt flakes, or to taste
½ tsp cumin seeds, slightly crushed, or sesame seeds
4 tbsp single, whipping or double cream

Combine the flour and sugar in a mixing bowl. Cut the butter into flakes and add to the bowl, then rub into the flour using the tips of your fingers until the mixture looks like fine, sandy crumbs.

Stir in the salt and seeds, then make a well in the centre of the mixture. Pour the cream and 3 tablespoons cold water into the well and gradually stir in the dry ingredients, using a round-bladed knife, adding more water a teaspoon at time until the mixture comes together to make a soft but not sticky dough.

Gently knead the dough in the bowl for a few seconds until it forms a smooth ball, then cover the bowl and leave at room temperature for 30 minutes to allow the dough to relax.

When ready to bake, line two baking sheets with baking paper and preheat the oven to 180°C.

Lightly dust the worktop and your rolling pin with flour. Cut the dough in half and roll out one portion to a thin sheet about 30 x 20cm – it doesn't need to be too neat. Prick the dough all over with a fork, then roll the dough around the rolling pin and lift it onto the baking sheet. Using a pizza wheel cutter or a large sharp knife, trim off the ragged edges (a ruler helps here), then cut the sheet into squares or rectangles. They may puff slightly in the oven and shrink slightly rather than expand, so you don't need to separate them. Repeat with the second portion of dough.

Bake for 14–18 minutes until golden and crisp – check after 12 minutes and rotate the baking sheets if necessary so they colour evenly.

Leave the crackers on the sheets for a couple of minutes, then transfer to a wire rack to cool.

When completely cold, store in an airtight container and eat within a week.

Index

Note: page numbers in **bold** refer to recipe illustrations.

almond (blanched)
   chocolate-dipped crescents 94
   cinnamon and raisin biscotti 122–3
   cinnamon sandies 16–17
   florentines 70–2, **71**
   raspberry crumbles 118–19
   snowy almond crescents 93–4
   toasted almond and fig biscotti 126–8
almond (flaked)
   German almond and honey squares 108–10, **109**
   macaroons – British tea-room style **83**, 84
almond (ground)
   lebkuchen 78–80, **81**
   macaroons – British tea-room style **83**, 84
   ricciarelli 85–6
Anzac biscuits 14–15

baking sheets, lining 10
bars 101–19
biscotti 121–33
   cheese 150–1
   cinnamon and raisin 122–3
   pistachio 124–5, **125**
   sea salt praline 131–3, **133**
   toasted almond and fig 126–8
   triple chocolate 129–30
black olive palmiers 144, **145**
black pepper
   lebkuchen 78–80, **81**
   polenta cracked black pepper crackers 146–7
   Parmesan palmiers 143–4
   sage and pecan biscuits 148–9, **149**
blue cheese: sage and pecan biscuits 148–9, **149**
blueberry: granola bars 111–12
bran mix: wheaten biscuits 20–2
brandy
   brandy snaps 76–7, 77
   rum and raisin tiffin 107
   snowy almond crescents 93–4
buckwheat flower: The National Trust's double choc, pistachio and sea salt cookies 58–9, **59**

caraway seed: Shrewsbury biscuits 98
cardamom: lebkuchen 78–80, **81**
Carnation Caramel: easy millionaire's shortbread 102–3
cayenne pepper
   cheese biscotti 150–1
   Parmesan palmiers 143–4
cheese
   cheese biscotti 150–1
   cheese Marmite walnut coins 136–7
   cheese shortbread 138
   Parmesan palmiers 143–4
   sage and pecan biscuits 148–9, **149**
cherry, sour
   florentines 70–2, **71**
   granola bars 111–12
   pistachio biscotti 124–5, **125**
   West Country Easter biscuits 97–8, **99**
   white chocolate, sour cherry and pistachio cookies 62–3
chilli
   savoury wheaten biscuits 22
   white chocolate, pine nut and chilli cookies 66–7
chocolate 10, 45–67
   chocolate chip vanilla cookies **46**, 48
   chocolate chip cookies 46–9, **46**
   chocolate glaze 79–80, **81**
   chocolate oaties 56–7
   chocolate shortbread fingers 43
   chocolate wheaten biscuits 22

chocolate-dipped
  brandy snaps 77
chocolate-dipped
  crescents 94
coconut kisses 89–90
dark chocolate crackles
  50–1
double chocolate chip
  cookies **46**, 47
double chocolate twists
  52–3, **53**
easy millionaire's
  shortbread 102–3
florentines 70–2, **71**
French chocolate
  fingers 54–5
ganache filling 87–8
gingerbread people
  73–5, **75**
granola bars 111–12
lebkuchen 78–80,
  81
melting 10
mocha kisses 91–2
party cookies 49
the richest chocolate
  biscuits 64–5
speckled shortbread
  43
The National Trust's
  double choc,
  pistachio and sea salt
  cookies 58–9, **59**
tiffin 106–7
toasted pecan
  chocolate macarons
  87–8
triple chocolate biscotti
  129–30
walnut chocolate
  crumbles 60–1
white chocolate, pine
  nut and chilli cookies
  66–7

white chocolate, sour
  cherry and pistachio
  cookies 62–3
chocolate spread:
  Viennese whirls 95–6
cinnamon
  cinnamon and raisin
    biscotti 122–3
  cinnamon sandies
    16–17
  Cragside Crackles
    23–4
  gingerbread people
    73–5, **75**
  granola bars 111–12
  lebkuchen 78–80,
    81
  oat and raisin cookies
    34–5
  sweet palmiers 144
  West Country Easter
    biscuits 97–8, **99**
cloves: lebkuchen 78–80,
  81
coconut (desiccated)
  Anzac biscuits 14–15
  coconut kisses 89–90
coffee
  mocha kisses 91–2
  the richest chocolate
    biscuits 64–5
cookies
  chocolate chip vanilla
    cookies **46**, 48
  chocolate chip cookies
    46–9, **46**
  chocolate-dipped
    crescents 94
  dark chocolate crackles
    50–1
  double chocolate chip
    cookies **46**, 47
  lemon poppy seed
    cookies 29–30, **31**

maple pecan cookies
  32–3
oat and raisin cookies
  34–5
party cookies 49
snowy almond
  crescents 93–4
The National Trust's
  double choc,
  pistachio and sea salt
  cookies 58–9, **59**
white chocolate, pine
  nut and chilli cookies
  66–7
white chocolate, sour
  cherry and pistachio
  cookies 62–3
cornflour
  custard 89–90
  Demerara shortbread
    rounds 42–3
  double chocolate twists
    52–3, **53**
  macaroons – British
    tea-room style **83**,
    84
  petticoat tails 39–40,
    41
  Viennese whirls 95–6,
    96
Cornish fairings 18–19
crackers
  polenta cracked black
    pepper 146–7
  olive oil thins with
    rosemary, za'atar or
    dukkah 141–2
  wholemeal cream
    152–3
Cragside Crackles 23–4
cranberry (dried)
  granola bars 111–12
  West Country Easter
    biscuits 97–8, **99**

cream
  florentines 70–2, **71**
  ganache filling 87–8
  German almond and honey squares 108–10, **109**
  wholemeal cream crackers 152–3
creaming method 38
crumbles
  raspberry crumbles 118–19
  walnut chocolate crumbles 60–1
crystallised fruit: florentines 70–2, **71**
cumin seed: wholemeal cream crackers 152–3
custard: coconut kisses 89–90

dark muscovado sugar
  gingerbread people 73–5, **75**
  lebkuchen 78–80, **81**
  oat and raisin cookies 34–5
  raspberry crumbles 118–19
  wheaten biscuits 20–2
Demerara sugar
  Demerara shortbread rounds 42–3
  florentines 70–2, **71**
  walnut chocolate crumbles 60–1
digestive biscuits *see* wheaten biscuits
dried fruit
  gingerbread people 73–5, **75**
  tiffin 106–7
  see also cherry, sour; cranberry (dried); fig; raisin(s); sultana(s)
dukkah: olive oil thins with 141–2

Easter biscuits: West Country 97–8, **99**
egg 9
  cheese biscotti 150–1
  chocolate chip vanilla cookies **46**, 48
  chocolate oaties 56–7
  cinnamon and raisin biscotti 122–3
  coconut kisses 89–90
  Cragside Crackles 23–4
  custard 89–90
  dark chocolate crackles 50–1
  double chocolate chip cookies **46**, 47
  double chocolate twists 52–3, **53**
  French sablés 25–6, **26**
  German almond and honey squares 108–10, **109**
  gingerbread people 73–5, **75**
  glaze 79–80, **81**
  jammy thumbprints 27–8
  lemon poppy seed cookies 29–30, **31**
  lemon squares 115–16, **117**
  macaroons – British tea-room style **83**, 84
  mocha kisses 91–2
  oat and raisin cookies 34–5
  old-fashioned double ginger snaps 36–7
  party cookies 49
  pistachio biscotti 124–5, **125**
  ricciarelli 85–6
  the richest chocolate biscuits 64–5
  sage and pecan biscuits 148–9, **149**
  sea salt praline biscotti 131–3, **133**
  The National Trust's double choc, pistachio and sea salt cookies 58–9, **59**
  toasted almond and fig biscotti 126–8
  toasted pecan chocolate macarons 87–8
  triple chocolate biscotti 129–30
  walnut chocolate crumbles 60–1
  West Country Easter biscuits 97–8, **99**
  white chocolate, pine nut and chilli cookies 66–7
  white chocolate, sour cherry and pistachio cookies 62–3

fairings: Cornish 18–19
fig: toasted almond and fig biscotti 126–8
fingers
  chocolate shortbread fingers 43
  French chocolate fingers 54–5
flapjack: sticky 104–5, **105**

florentines 70–2, **71**
French sablés 25–6, **26**
fudge layer 102–3

ganache filling 87–8
garam masala: savoury wheaten biscuits 22
German almond and honey squares 108–10, **109**
ginger
   brandy snaps 76–7, **77**
   Cornish fairings 18–19
   Cragside Crackles 23–4
   ginger shortbread 43
   gingerbread people 73–5, **75**
   Grasmere ginger shortbread 113–14
   lebkuchen 78–80, **81**
   old-fashioned double ginger snaps 36–7
   tiffin 106–7
glacé icing 73–5, **75**
glazes 23–4, 25–6, 79–80, **81**
gluten free (GF) 10
   granola bars 111–12
   macaroons 82–6
   oatcakes 139–40
   Parmesan palmiers 143–4
   sticky flapjacks 104–5, **105**
   The National Trust's double choc, pistachio and sea salt cookies 58–9, **59**
   tiffin 106–7
golden syrup
   Anzac biscuits 14–15
   brandy snaps 76–7, **77**
   Cornish fairings 18–19

gingerbread people 73–5, **75**
old-fashioned double ginger snaps 36–7
sticky flapjacks 104–5, **105**
tiffin 106–7
Grana Padano cheese
   cheese biscotti 150–1
   cheese Marmite walnut coins 136–7
   cheese shortbread 138
   Parmesan palmiers 143–4
granola bars 111–12
Grasmere ginger shortbread 113–14

hazelnut
   easy millionaire's shortbread 102–3
   florentines 70–2, **71**
   raspberry crumbles 118–19
   sea salt praline biscotti 131–3, **133**
honey
   German almond and honey squares 108–10, **109**
   lebkuchen 78–80, **81**

icing: glacé 73–5, **75**

jam
   jammy thumbprints 27–8
   raspberry crumbles 118–19
   Viennese whirls 95–6, **96**

kitchen equipment 10, 11

lavender rounds 43
lebkuchen 78–80, **81**
lemon
   gingerbread people 73–5, **75**
   lebkuchen 78–80, **81**
   lemon pistachio squares 116
   lemon poppy seed cookies 29–30, **31**
   lemon squares 115–16, **117**
   West Country Easter biscuits 97–8, **99**
light muscovado sugar
   chocolate chip vanilla cookies **46**, 48
   chocolate oaties 56–7
   Cragside Crackles 23–4
   dark chocolate crackles 50–1
   double chocolate chip cookies **46**, 47
   easy millionaire's shortbread 102–3
   Grasmere ginger shortbread 113–14
   oat and raisin cookies 34–5
   oatcakes 139–40
   maple pecan cookies 32–3
   party cookies 49
   sticky flapjacks 104–5, **105**
   The National Trust's double choc, pistachio and sea salt cookies 58–9, **59**
   triple chocolate biscotti 129–30

white chocolate, pine nut and chilli cookies 66–7
white chocolate, sour cherry and pistachio cookies 62–3

macarons 82–3
  toasted pecan chocolate macarons 87–8
macaroons 82–90, **83**
  coconut kisses 89–90
  macaroons – British tea-room style **83**, 84
  ricciarelli 85–6
maple syrup
  granola bars 111–12
  maple pecan cookies 32–3
Marmite: cheese Marmite walnut coins 136–7
millionaire's shortbread: easy 102–3
mixed spice
  Cornish fairings 18–19
  Cragside Crackles 23–4
  gingerbread people 73–5, **75**
  lebkuchen 78–80, **81**
  oat and raisin cookies 34–5
  West Country Easter biscuits 97–8, **99**
mocha kisses 91–2
mustard: Parmesan palmiers 143–4

National Trust's double choc, pistachio and sea salt cookies, The 58–9, **59**

nutmeg
  easy millionaire's shortbread 102–3
  lebkuchen 78–80, **81**
  raspberry crumbles 118–19
  Shrewsbury biscuits 98
nut(s) 10
  chocolate oaties 56–7
  florentines 70–2, **71**
  gingerbread people 73–5, **75**
  granola bars 111–12
  raspberry crumbles 118–19
  sticky flapjacks 104–5, 105
  tiffin 106–7
  see also almond; hazelnut; pecan; pine nut; pistachio; walnut

oatcakes 139–40
oatmeal
  Grasmere ginger shortbread 113–14
  oatcakes 139–40
  wheaten biscuits 20–2
oat(s) (porridge) 9
  Anzac biscuits 14–15
  chocolate oaties 56–7
  Cragside Crackles 23–4
  granola bars 111–12
  jammy thumbprints 27–8
  oat and raisin cookies 34–5
  party cookies 49
  raspberry crumbles 118–19
  sticky flapjacks 104–5, **105**

olive oil
  granola bars 111–12
  lemon poppy seed cookies 29–30, **31**
  olive oil thins with rosemary, za'atar or dukkah 141–2
  polenta cracked black pepper crackers 146–7
olive(s): black olive palmiers 144, **145**
orange zest
  lebkuchen 78–80, **81**
  ricciarelli 85–6
  triple chocolate biscotti 129–30
oven temperatures 11
oven thermometers 11

palmiers **145**
  black olive 144, **145**
  Parmesan 143–4
  sweet 144
paprika
  cheese biscotti 150–1
  Parmesan palmiers 143–4
Parmesan cheese
  cheese biscotti 150–1
  cheese Marmite walnut coins 136–7
  cheese shortbread 138
  Parmesan palmiers 143–4
party cookies 49
pecan nut
  double chocolate chip cookies **46**, 47
  maple pecan cookies 32–3

sage and pecan biscuits
  148–9, **149**
toasted pecan
  chocolate macarons
  87–8
peel (crystallised):
  florentines 70–2, **71**
peel (mixed): Cornish
  fairings 18–19
petticoat tails 39–40, **41**
pine nut: white chocolate,
  pine nut and chilli
  cookies 66–7
pistachio
  florentines 70–2, **71**
  lemon pistachio
    squares 116
  pistachio biscotti
    124–5, **125**
  pistachio shortbread
    43
  The National Trust's
    double choc,
    pistachio and sea salt
    cookies 58–9, **59**
  white chocolate, sour
    cherry and pistachio
    cookies 62–3
polenta
  Demerara shortbread
    rounds 42–3
  polenta cracked black
    pepper crackers
    146–7
poppy seed: lemon poppy
  seed cookies 29–30, **31**
praline: sea salt praline
  biscotti 131–3, **133**
puff pastry: Parmesan
  palmiers 143–4
puffed rice breakfast
  cereal: granola bars
  111–12

raisin(s)
  cinnamon and raisin
    biscotti 122–3
  granola bars 111–12
  oat and raisin cookies
    34–5
  rum and raisin tiffin
    107
  sticky flapjacks 104–5,
    105
  West Country Easter
    biscuits 97–8, **99**
raspberry crumbles
  118–19
ricciarelli – oval soft-style
  macaroons from Siena
  85–6
rice flour: Demerara
  shortbread rounds 42–3
rosemary: olive oil thins
  with 141–2
rosewater: Shrewsbury
  biscuits 98
rum and raisin tiffin 107

sablés: French 25–6, **26**
sage and pecan biscuits
  148–9, **149**
sandies: cinnamon 16–17
savoury biscuits 22,
  135–53
Scottish shortbread 38–43
sea salt
  sea salt praline biscotti
    131–3, **133**
  The National Trust's
    double choc,
    pistachio and sea salt
    cookies 58–9, **59**
seed(s)
  granola bars 111–12
  see also caraway seed;
    poppy seed; sesame
    seed

sesame seed
  cheese Marmite walnut
    coins 136–7
  olive oil thins with
    rosemary, za'atar or
    dukkah 141–2
  polenta cracked black
    pepper crackers
    146–7
  wholemeal cream
    crackers 152–3
shortbread
  cheese shortbread 138
  Demerara shortbread
    rounds 42–3
  easy millionaire's
    shortbread 102–3
  Grasmere ginger
    shortbread 113–14
  lemon squares 115–16,
    117
  petticoat tails 39–40,
    41
  Scottish shortbread
    38–43, **41**
Shrewsbury biscuits 98
Smarties: party cookies 49
snowy almond crescents
  93–4
spices 10
  see also mixed spice
squares 101–19
sultana(s)
  florentines 70–2, **71**
  West Country Easter
    biscuits 97–8, **99**
sweet palmiers 144

thumbprints: jammy 27–8
tiffin 106–7
  rum and raisin 107
Tabasco: white chocolate,
  pine nut and chilli
  cookies 66–7

vanilla
- chocolate chip vanilla cookies **46**, 48
- chocolate oaties 56–7
- cinnamon and raisin biscotti 122–3
- Cragside Crackles 23–4
- custard 89–90
- dark chocolate crackles 50–1
- double chocolate twists 52–3, **53**
- French chocolate fingers 54–5
- French sablés 25–6, **26**
- German almond and honey squares 108–10, **109**
- oat and raisin cookies 34–5
- party cookies 49
- The National Trust's double choc, pistachio and sea salt cookies 58–9, **59**
- vanilla rounds 43
- Viennese whirls 95–6, **96**

walnut
- cheese biscotti 150–1
- cheese Marmite walnut coins 136–7
- chocolate chip vanilla cookies **46**, 48
- double chocolate chip cookies **46**, 47
- florentines 70–2, **71**
- mocha kisses 91–2
- oat and raisin cookies 34–5
- walnut chocolate crumbles 60–1
- West Country Easter biscuits 97–8, **99**
- wheaten biscuits 20–2
- walnut chocolate crumbles 60–1
- white chocolate, pine nut and chilli cookies 66–7
- white chocolate, sour cherry and pistachio cookies 62–3
- Viennese whirls 95–6, **96**

white chocolate
- chocolate biscuits 22
- chocolate crumbles 60–1
- chocolate-dipped crescents 94
- chocolate oaties 56–7
- double chocolate twists 52–3, **53**
- French chocolate fingers 54–5
- toasted pecan chocolate macarons 87–8
- triple chocolate biscotti 129–30
- walnut chocolate crumbles 60–1
- white chocolate, pine nut and chilli cookies 66–7
- white chocolate, sour cherry and pistachio cookies 62–3
- wholemeal cream crackers 152–3

za'atar: olive oil thins with 141–2

Acknowledgements

I would like to thank the National Trust, and their editor Ruby Tyler, along with the volunteer guides and gardeners, for helping me with this project.

I have been immensely lucky to work with the marvellous team at HarperCollins: Peter Taylor and the ever-patient David Salmo; stellar editor Maggie Ramsay; artist Louise Morgan; designers James Hunter and Geoff Borin; proofreader Gill Knappett; indexer Lisa Footitt – thank you all.

And huge thanks to my agent and friend Barbara Levy; biscuit aficionados Alan, Daniel, Stevie, and my Hertz family, plus all those friends who volunteered to taste test.